CONTROLLING FEDERAL PRISON COSTS

CONTROLLING FEDERAL PRISON COSTS

GREGORY N. BERRITAS
EDITOR

Nova Science Publishers, Inc.
New York

For permission to use material from this book please contact us:
Telephone 631-231-7269; Fax 631-231-8175
Web Site: http://www.novapublishers.com

LIBRARY OF CONGRESS CATALOGING-IN-PUBLICATION DATA

Available Upon Request

ISBN: 978-1-60692-650-5

Published by Nova Science Publishers, Inc. ✝ New York

Contents

PREFACE

Over the last 10 years, the cost to confine federal Bureau of Prison (BOP) inmates in non-BOP facilities has nearly tripled from about $250 million in fiscal year 1996 to about $700 million in fiscal year 2006. Proponents of using contractors to operate prisons claim it can save money; others question whether contracting is a cost-effective alternative. This book discusses the feasibility and implications of comparing the costs for confining federal inmates in low and minimum security BOP facilities with those managed by private firms for BOP.

In: Controlling Federal Prison Costs
Editor: Gregory N. Berritas
ISBN 978-1-60692-650-5

Chapter 1

COST OF PRISONS*

ABBREVIATIONS

BOP	Federal Bureau of Prisons
FAR	Federal Acquisition Regulation
IGA	intergovernmental agreement
NIJ	National Institute of Justice
OMB	Office of Management and Budget

October 5, 2007

The Honorable Barbara A. Mikulski
Chair
The Honorable Richard C. Shelby
Ranking Member
Subcommittee on Commerce, Justice,
Science, and Related Agencies Committee on Appropriations
United States Senate
The Honorable Alan B. Mollohan

---

* Excerpeted from GAO Report to the Subcommittees on Commerce, Justice, and Science, Senate and House Appropriations Committees, dated October 2007.

Chairman
The Honorable Rodney Frelinghuysen
Ranking Member
Subcommittee on Commerce, Justice, Science, and Related Agencies
Committee on Appropriations
House of Representatives

At the end of fiscal year 2006, approximately 83,000 federal, adult male inmates within the Department of Justice's Federal Bureau of Prisons (BOP) were housed or confined in low or minimum security facilities, and in recent years BOP has relied on means other than building and operating its own facilities to confine many of these inmates, such as contracts with private sector firms. BOP's operating budget nearly doubled over the last decade from approximately $2.6 billion in fiscal year 1996 to just under $5 billion in fiscal year 2006. In fiscal year 1996, BOP received approximately $250 million of its $2.6 billion for contract confinement, including confining inmates in facilities owned and operated by private contractors and by state and local governments under intergovernmental agreements (IGA) with BOP [1]. By fiscal year 2006, the amount for contract confinement, including the cost of confining about 19,000 inmates housed in private and IGA facilities, had nearly tripled to $700 million of BOP's $5 billion operating budget.

There has been an ongoing debate over the privatization of prisons, that is, contracting for the management of prisons by private firms, whether theprisons are owned by the private sector or by the government. In particular, proponents of privatization claim it can save money without reducing the levels or quality of service such as safety and security (i.e., levels of safety and security for staff, inmates, and the general public), whereas others have questioned whether privatization is a cost-effective alternative to publicly run facilities. Federal guidance from the Office of Management and Budget (OMB) requires that economic and cost comparison analyses be conducted to demonstrate the benefits of privatization, including how it would reduce the government's long-term costs. BOP's use of contracting to meet inmate bed space needs at low and minimum security facilities, in particular, has generated significant interest in the comparative costs of confining federal inmates in BOP, private, and IGA facilities. Conference Report 109-272, accompanying the Science, State, Justice, Commerce, and Related Agencies Appropriations Act of 2006, [2] directed GAO to compare the costs of confining federal inmates in BOP, private, and IGA low and minimum security facilities.

Regarding IGA facilities, BOP has used IGAs for a number of years to confine low and minimum security inmates on a short term basis—less than 45 days—for the purposes of transferring them between facilities or as halfway houses when inmates are released from prison. These IGAs are in hundreds of locations throughout the country. However, according to BOP officials, over time four of the IGAs—located in western Texas, in the cities of Big Spring and Eden, Texas, and Garza County and Reeves County, Texas—evolved into facilities confining inmates on a long-term basis, similar to BOP-owned and -operated low and minimum security facilities. BOP officials told us that these four facilities confined approximately 83 percent of BOP's total IGA inmate population. During the course of our review, BOP did not renew the four Texas IGAs. Instead, BOP awarded five contracts to confine inmates in facilities with approximately 10,000 beds, which are about 3,000 more beds than the capacity provided under the four IGAs [3]. According to BOP officials, BOP chose to compete the bed space associated with these former agreements partly because the four Texas facilities outgrew their original purpose of confining small populations for short periods of time. BOP officials also stated that acquiring bed space via contracts rather than IGAs enhances their ability to oversee operations at the facilities. Because BOP no longer plans to use IGAs to confine inmates on a long-term basis, we shifted the focus of our review to BOP and private facilities only. Also, we did not include the five new contracts in the scope of our review because no federal inmates were housed under the new contract arrangements during fiscal years 2002 through 2006, the period covered by our review.

This report discusses the feasibility of comparing the cost of confining inmates in low and minimum security facilities owned and operated by BOP with the cost of confining these inmates in private facilities and the implications this has for making decisions on low and minimum security confinement.

To address this objective, we reviewed applicable laws, regulations, and studies on BOP programs, prison management, and contracting requirements [4]. We also examined available BOP and private facility documents on the management of low and minimum security facilities. In addition, we met with BOP officials and worked with them to identify potential BOP and private facilities that could be compared considering basic criteria, including inmate gender (male or female inmates, assuming that costs for programs and services might be different depending on gender) and whether cost data might be available on the individual facility level for a 5-year period covering fiscal years 2002 through 2006 [5]. Our discussions with BOP officials resulted in the selection of 34 low and minimum security facilities managed by BOP and private operators that confined federally sentenced male inmates on a long-term basis over the 5-

year period. Specifically, we focused on (1) 27 BOP-owned and -operated low and minimum security facilities that are not on the same campus as medium and high security prisons (BOP does not isolate the costs of operating individual low and minimum security facilities located on the same campus with high and medium security facilities), and (2) 7 facilities operated by private firms under contract to BOP.

Once we selected facilities, we interviewed BOP officials in Washington, D.C. and private contractors at their corporate headquarters to determine what data on prison costs and characteristics would be available. Where possible, we gathered and analyzed available data on the facilities and examined whether the data would lend themselves to a comparison based, in part, on key factors—such as similar facility characteristics and levels of service—needed to do a methodologically sound comparison as outlined in our 1996 report that provides lessons learned for comparisons of private and public correctional facilities [6]. In addition, we examined BOP efforts within the context of OMB requirements for capital planning and space acquisition. We also met with OMB staff responsible for BOP budget review and preparation to discuss BOP's efforts to acquire space to confine inmates in low and minimum security facilities in order to determine what information BOP provides OMB on capital investments, how this information is used to inform decisions, and what additional information OMB needs to make informed decisions. In addition, we met with officials from the Department of Justice's National Institute of Justice (NIJ) to discuss NIJ's current and past work on prison privatization and we met with experts from Florida State University College of Criminology and Criminal Justice and from the JFA Institute—a nonprofit agency conducting justice and corrections research for effective policy making— to further our understanding about prisons and the complexities of comparing the cost of operating private and public prisons. Appendix I contains more detailed information on our scope and methodology.

We conducted our work from May 2006 through August 2007 in accordance with generally accepted government auditing standards.

Results in Brief

It is not currently feasible to conduct a methodologically sound cost comparison of BOP and private low and minimum security facilities because these facilities differ in several characteristics and BOP does not collect comparable data to determine the impact of these differences on cost. Our past work has shown that generally accepted evaluation criteria for any comparative study of private and public prisons call for the comparison to be based not just on operational costs, but on a variety of factors including selection of facilities with similar characteristics (i.e., staffing levels and programs offered) and quality of service. This is to ensure that cost comparison analyses either compare similar facilities or can account for differences in order to address whether facilities operating at lower costs can provide the same or better levels of service as those operating at higher costs. However, according to BOP officials andprivate contractors, facilities differed in characteristics and in quality of service. Although BOP collects and maintains characteristic data on its own low and minimum security facilities, BOP does not gather data on private contract facilities that would enable us or them to account or adjust for any differences. While private contractors told us that they maintain some data for their records, these officials said that the data are not readily available or in a format that would enable a methodologically sound cost comparison at this time. According to BOP officials and private contractors,

- In terms of facility characteristics, BOP facilities generally confine U.S. citizens, and programs are designed to teach inmates skills that they can use when they are released so as to avoid returning to prison. By contrast, private facilities primarily confine criminal aliens—non-U.S. citizens or foreign nationals who are serving time for a U.S. federal conviction. Programs that focus on preventing returns to prison are not required of private facilities because criminal aliens are released for removal from the country and are not expected to return to U.S. communities or BOP custody.
- BOP does not require private facility data comparable to what it maintains for its own facilities with regard to safety and security issues and, consequently, a facility's quality of service. These include data on the number of inmates attended to by health care professionals due to misconduct, staff turnover rates, and the experience level of the staff.

BOP does not collect comparable data on private facilities needed to conduct a methodologically sound cost comparison with BOP low and minimum security facilities because (1) federal regulations do not require BOP to do so when selecting among competing contractors, and (2) according to BOP officials, collecting additional facility characteristic and quality of service data could add costs to contracts. Regarding the latter, BOP's Senior Deputy Assistant Director stated that private contractors might charge higher contract prices as a result of having to collect and provide this information but that BOP has not determined what these additional costs would be. BOP officials told us they are committed to contracting to confine inmates in low and minimum security facilities. They said that their construction priority is medium and high security facilities because inmates in medium and high security facilities are at higher risk in terms of their behavior (i.e., rates of misconduct, assaults, and history of violence) and private contractors have yet to demonstrate the ability to handle these higher security populations. According to BOPofficials, because of its commitment to contracting, BOP has not recently considered, nor does it plan to evaluate contracting in relation to other alternatives for inmates confined in low and minimum security facilities. These alternatives can include constructing new BOP low and minimum security facilities, acquiring and using excess military properties, or expanding or renovating existing BOP facilities.

While BOP does not need to collect comparable data for selecting among contractors, the purpose of analyzing these data is to evaluate and justify whether confining inmates in private facilities is more cost-effective than these other confinement alternatives. In fact, OMB requires agencies to consider and weigh various alternatives using analyses, such as benefit- cost or cost-effectiveness analyses, when making decisions about the acquisition of capital assets, such as office buildings, hospitals, schools, and prisons [7]. According to OMB, selecting alternatives to meet space requirements without adequate analysis by federal agencies has resulted in higher costs than anticipated. Additionally, OMB staff stated that they need more and better cost comparison information on the various alternatives for BOP's low and minimum security facilities to help better understand the long-term costs and benefits of owning versus the short- term costs and benefits of privatization. These analyses are especially important because BOP officials stated that the population for these facilities continues to grow. Without such analyses, it is difficult to know whether BOP is deciding on the most cost-effective alternative for acquiring low and minimum security facilities to confine inmates, including whether to contract, build, or expand.

Recognizing that there is a cost associated with gathering and analyzing additional data needed to compare costs across BOP and private facilities, we are making one recommendation designed to help BOP evaluate alternatives for confining inmates in low and minimum security facilities. We are recommending that the Attorney General direct the Director of BOP to develop a cost-effective way to collect comparable data across BOP and private low and minimum security facilities confining inmates under BOP's custody, and design and conduct methodologically sound analyses that compare the cost of confining inmates in these facilities in order to consider contracting among other alternatives for low and minimum security confinement, consistent with OMB requirements.

BOP disagreed with our recommendation and stated that it does not own or operate facilities to house solely criminal aliens. BOP also said it does not expect to receive funding to construct such low security facilities. Therefore, BOP does not believe there is value in developing data collection methods to compare costs of confining these inmates in private facilities with other alternatives for confining inmates. BOP further commented that, through open competition, it has been able to determine a fair and reasonable price for its existing contracts and said that requiring contractors to provide specific comparable data would have the potential to increase current contract costs at a time when BOP is facing budget constraints. BOP also noted that it believes a 2005 study conducted for BOP by a private contractor has already met the intent of our recommendation because the study compares the cost of operating a government-owned, contractor-operated facility in Taft, California, with other low security BOP facilities [8].

We agree that full and open competition can establish fair and reasonable costs for services provided by contractors. However, our recommendation is about selecting the most cost-effective alternative for confining inmates, not about selecting among contractors as the only alternative. We believe that developing data collection methods to determine the costs of confining inmates in low and minimum security facilities—regardless of whether those facilities are owned and operated by BOP or a contractor and regardless of whether the facility confines criminal aliens, U.S. citizens, or both—is critical to BOP's ability to evaluate the cost- effectiveness of contracting compared to other alternatives for confining inmates, such as constructing a new facility or modifying existing facilities. Absent this evaluation, key decision makers, including BOP managers, OMB, and Congress, are not positioned to have the information needed to make the most cost-effective investment decisions.

We agree that requiring contractors to provide data so that BOP can conduct a comparison has the potential of increasing contract costs, but BOP has not assessed what the costs of collecting the data would be or whether the costs would outweigh the benefit of being able to determine the most cost- effective alternative for confining inmates in low and minimum security facilities.

Finally, we disagree that BOP has met the intent of our recommendation via the study referenced by BOP because it does not compare the costs of various alternatives for confining inmates in low and minimum security facilities, as we recommended.

BACKGROUND

BOP was established in 1930 to provide progressive and humane care for federal inmates in the 11 federal prisons in operation at the time. Since then, BOP's mission has evolved into protecting society by controlling offenders in the controlled environments of prisons and community-based facilities that are safe, humane, cost-efficient, and appropriately secure and that provide work and other self-improvement opportunities to assist offenders in becoming law-abiding citizens.

At the end of fiscal year 2006, there were over 114 federal prison facilities located throughout the country at four primary security levels—minimum, low, medium, and high. BOP facilities are given a security designation based on the level of security and staff supervision the facility is able to provide.

According to BOP, minimum security facilities, also known as Federal Prison Camps, have dormitory housing and limited or no perimeter fencing; low security Federal Correctional Institutions have double-fenced perimeters and mostly dormitory or cubicle housing; medium security Federal Correctional Institutions have strengthened perimeters (often double fences with electronic detection systems) where inmates are mostly confined to prison cells; and high security institutions, also known as United States Penitentiaries, have highly secured perimeters (featuring walls or reinforced fences) and multiple- and single-occupant cell housing. BOP also maintains administrative facilities, which are institutions with special missions, such as the detention of pretrial offenders; [9] the treatment of inmates with serious or chronic medical problems; or the containment of extremely dangerous, violent, or escape- prone inmates. Administrative facilities are capable of holding inmates at all security levels.

According to BOP population data, at the end of fiscal year 2006, BOP's total inmate population was approximately 193,000 inmates, of which about 43 percent, or 83,000, were long-term, adult male inmates confined in BOP, private, or IGA low and minimum security facilities.

About 52,000 (27 percent) of the total inmates were confined in medium security facilities, and approximately 18,000 (about 9 percent) were in high security facilities. Additionally, approximately 21 percent of the 193,000 total inmates, or 40,000 inmates, were females, juveniles, inmates in halfway houses, inmates in home confinement, or inmates confined in BOP's administrative facilities. See figure 1 for a breakout of these populations.

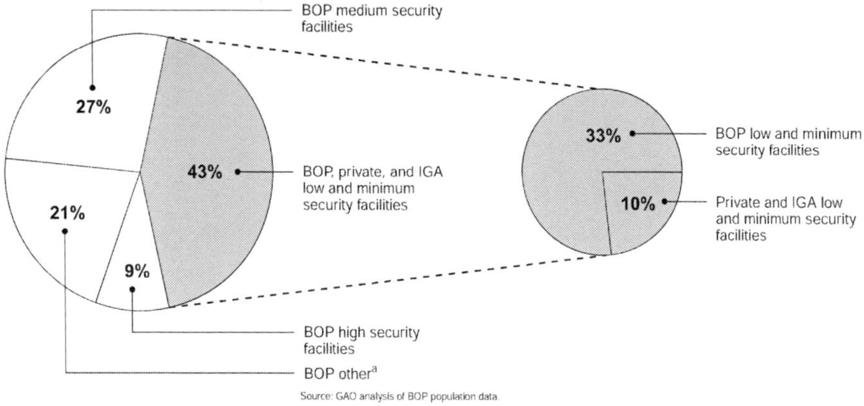

Source: GAO analysis of BOP population data.

[a]BOP other includes females, juveniles, inmates in halfway houses, inmates in home confinement, or inmates confined in BOP's administrative facilities (i.e., medical facilities or detention facilities.

Figure 1. BOP Inmate Population at the End of Fiscal Year 2006.

BOP Lacks Data Needed to Perform a Methodologically Sound Cost Comparison and Is Not Positioned to Evaluate Alternatives for Confining Inmates in Low and Minimum Security Facilities

A methodologically sound cost comparison analysis of BOP and private low and minimum security facilities is not currently feasible because BOP does not gather data from private facilities that are comparable to the data collected on BOP facilities. BOP is not required under federal contracting regulations to gather data that would enable a comparison, and although BOP has not evaluated the cost of collecting additional information, BOP officials maintain that it could increase the price contractors charge BOP for contract services.

However, without comparable data, BOP is not able to analyze and justify whether confining inmates in private facilities would be more cost-effective than other confinement alternatives such as constructing new BOP facilities or renovating existing BOP facilities.

Such an analysis would be consistent with OMB requirements, which call for agencies to identify and evaluate various alternatives when making decisions about the acquisition of capital assets (e.g., office buildings, hospitals, schools, and prisons).

A Cost Comparison Is Not Currently Feasible because BOP Lacks Data Needed to Perform a Methodologically Sound Comparison

We determined that it is not currently feasible to compare the cost of confining male federal inmates in low and minimum security BOP and private facilities because data needed for a methodologically sound comparison are not currently available. Our review of BOP documentation showed that BOP collects basic cost data on a per inmate basis across BOP and private facilities. For BOP-owned and -operated facilities, BOP maintains per inmate costs that include salaries, employee benefits, equipment, and utilities. For private facilities, BOP maintains the negotiated per inmate contract price, award fees, and deductions made as a result of the performance-based contract terms. However, these cost data are not sufficient for doing a methodologically sound cost comparison. As we reported in 1996, any comparative study of private and public prisons should not only be based on operational costs but also on an analysis of similar facilities—including the design, capacity, security level, and types of inmates and quality of service—and on sufficient statistical controls to measure and account for any differences among facilities [10]. Otherwise, any comparative analysis of operational costs could be skewed. For example, one study we reviewed as part of our 1996 report did not assess quality of service as part of the cost comparison between private and public facilities and, as a result, could not conclude whether the levels of service affected the differences in costs.

According to BOP officials and private contractors, BOP and private facilities have different characteristics and provide different levels of service. Thus, statistical methods would need to be used to account for these differences once cost data were collected to determine the impact they have on the operating cost of the facilities. Using guidelines established in our previous work, we sought to compare facilities with similar characteristics to ensure results of a comparison would not be skewed. However, we were unable to do so because the data needed to do the comparison were not available. BOP and private contracting officials reported that there are numerous differences among BOP and private facilities, including inmate population, program requirements, and economic differences within the different geographic locations of the facilities. According to BOP officials, private contractor facilities have fewer contractual requirements for programming, such as vocational training and release preparation courses, than BOP facilities, in part, because of the different types of inmates confined in the facilities. In general, BOP facilities confine U.S. citizens and programs are designed to teach inmates skills that they can use when they are released, such as job training skills, so as to help avoid their return to prison. By contrast, private facilities primarily confine criminal aliens—non-U.S. citizens or foreign nationals, who are serving time for a U.S. federal conviction. Programs that focus on preventing returns to prison are not required of private facilities because criminal aliens are released for removal from the country and are not expected to return to U.S. communities or BOP custody.

Given the differences with regard to facility characteristics, statistical techniques such as analyzing the extent to which characteristics— including program differences—vary among facilities, would have to be applied to strengthen conclusions of a cost comparison analysis. For example, if BOP facilities provide more programs for inmates than contractors do, then comparable data on the number and types of programs across all facilities would be needed to adjust for this difference in order to conclude how the difference in programs affect operating costs. BOP maintains data on its own low and minimum security facilities and collects some similar facility data on private facilities, including the age of the facility, the citizenship status of inmates, and inmate population. However, BOP does not maintain comparable data on various aspects ofprivate facilities, such as inmate-to-staff ratios, size of the facility, specific programs available to inmates, and whether inmates in private facilities are completing those programs. Because BOP does not maintain comparable data for private facilities on the differing facility characteristics that could affect costs, we could not determine the extent to which these facilities differed nor use statistical methods to determine the impact of these differences on costs. Since we could not control or adjust for such differences, the results of a cost comparison analysis conducted at this time would be skewed.

With regard to quality of service, BOP also lacks sufficient data on measurements of safety and security for inmates, staff, and the general public for a methodologically sound cost comparison of BOP and private facilities. As we reported in 1996, a cost comparison analysis should include not just operational costs but also an assessment of quality to ensure that if a contractor is operating at lower costs than BOP, it is providing the same or a better level of service. We attempted to review numerous quality of service data—such as data that measure safety and security—so that differences could be accounted for by comparing data on what is achieved by these services. However, according to officials in BOP's

Office of Research and Evaluation, BOP does not maintain data on private facilities that we could use to compare quality of service across the different facilities. This includes the number of grievances submitted by inmates, the number of inmates attended to by health care professionals due to misconduct, [11] staff turnover rates, and the experience level of the staff. As a result, we could not assess the trade-offs between the levels of services being offered and the costs of operating the facilities.

While the contract requirements for the private facilities direct contractors to maintain some data on inmates in BOP's central database system called SENTRY, [12] according to BOP officials, the data private contractors enter are not necessarily consistent with those data collected on BOP facilities, and BOP officials stated that they cannot attest to the reliability or validity of the private contractor data. For example, BOP officials and private contractors we spoke with stated that although private contractors are required to report incidences of misconduct to BOP, neither could confirm if the private contractor system for categorizing or tracking incidences of misconduct is consistent with BOP's misconduct categories [13]. BOP further reported that program data were not comparable. For example, according to BOP officials, private contractors reported that inmates completed the U.S. General Educational Development program, when the program actually completed by the inmates was a Mexican equivalent of the program. Additionally, private contractors we spoke with told us that they maintain some facility characteristic and quality of service data, but the data are not maintained in the same format as BOP facility data and are not readily available because they are only maintained in hard copies at some of the facilities contractors manage.

BOP officials provided two reasons why they do not collect or require contractors to collect comparable data that would facilitate a comparison of the cost of confining inmates in low and minimum security BOP and private facilities: (1) federal regulations do not require such data as a means for selecting among competing contractors, and (2) BOP believes collecting comparable data from contractors could add costs. However, BOP officials had not evaluated the probable amount of added costs.

When choosing among private contractors, federal regulations do not require BOP to collect comparable facility characteristic or quality of service information from private facilities. According to BOP officials, all BOP private contracts in our review are firm-fixed price and, under federal regulations for competing contracts, BOP does not need this information for technical evaluations of the proposals [14]. BOP officials added that during the acquisition process, BOP maintains data needed to evaluate proposed contract prices, such as the price to manage and operate each facility and the government's estimate of the price, in accordance with the Federal Acquisition Regulation (FAR). The FAR requires the contracting official to determine if proposed prices are fair and reasonable and further states that the performance of a cost analysis is not needed if there is adequate price competition [15]. In general, adequate price competition is established when two or more responsible parties independently submit prices for the solicitation that meet the government's requirements. The award is made to the party whose proposal represents the best value and there is no finding that the price of the other parties is unreasonable. In addition to price, the FAR recommends agencies evaluate one or more nonprice criteria, such as past performance and prior experience. However, agencies have broad discretion in the selection criteria and in determining the relative importance of each criterion. Consequently, the regulation does not require BOP to collect comparable data on various facility characteristics and quality of service measures needed to conduct a methodologically sound cost comparison.

Additionally, while BOP is concerned that the cost of contracts could increase if it were to require comparable data from private contractors because it would be beyond the scope of existing contract requirements, it has not evaluated the costs or benefits of acquiring the additional data. BOP's Senior Deputy Assistant Director and other BOP officials said they suspect that it is likely that private contractors would charge BOP a higher contract price if it required private contractors to meet additional requirements, such as providing data similar to those collected by BOP for its facilities. However, because BOP has not requested such data during the contract process or estimated the incremental costs and benefits of requiring comparable data from private facilities, BOP officials could not speak to the extent of the potential cost increase.

Although in the Department of Justice Fiscal Year 2003-2008 Strategic Plan BOP identified several alternatives for space acquisition, such as expanding or renovating existing facilities, acquiring military properties for prison use, contracting with private companies, and constructing new facilities, BOP officials stated that they do not consider all of these alternatives for confining inmates in low and minimum security facilities because they are committed to contracting with nonfederal entities for low and minimum security bed space.

Our past work has shown that over the long term, it is usually more cost-effective for an agency to own a facility than to lease one [16]. For example, we previously reported that for nine major operating lease acquisitions proposed by the General Services Administration—the central leasing agent for most federal agencies—construction would have been the least expensive option in eight cases and would have saved an estimated $126 million compared to two leasing options that spread payments out over time [17]. However, when funds for ownership are not available, leases become a more attractive option from the agency's budget perspective because they add much less to a single year's appropriation total than other alternatives. According to BOP officials, they consider alternatives for space acquisition only for medium and high security facilities, because medium and high security facilities are BOP's priority based on capacity needs. In addition to capacity needs, from BOP's perspective, inmates in medium and high security facilities are at higher risk in terms of their behavior (i.e., rates of misconduct, assaults, and history of violence) and private contractors have yet to demonstrate the ability to handle these higher security populations, so BOP has chosen to continue to confine the higher security inmates in BOP-owned and -operated facilities. As a result, BOP officials stated that they have not considered nor do they plan to consider alternatives besides contracting for low and minimum security facilities.

BOP Cannot Evaluate whether Privately Contracted Facilities Provide Better or Worse Value than Other Low and Minimum Security Confinement

AlternativesBecause BOP is not able to compare the cost of BOP and private facilities in a methodologically sound manner, it cannot determine if confining inmates in private facilities is more or less cost-effective than other confinement alternatives such as constructing and operating new BOP facilities, acquiring and using excess properties (i.e., former military bases), or expanding or renovating existing BOP facilities. OMB requires agencies to follow capital planning principles set forth in its *Capital Programming Guide* [18]. OMB's guide identifies the need for effectiveplanning and management of investments. Among other things, this guide articulates key principles agencies should follow when making decisions about the acquisition of capital assets such as prisons. The *Capital Programming Guide* requires that agencies consider as many alternatives as possible because, according to the guide, whenever the government lacks viable alternatives, it may lack a realistic basis to manage contract costs. Once a list of alternatives is established, the guide requires that agencies then compare those alternatives based on a systematic analysis of expected benefits and costs. The fundamental method for formal economic analysis is a benefit-cost analysis. OMB guidance on benefit-cost analyses can be found in OMB Circular A-94—a circular that helps agencies conduct a study on the benefits and costs of whether to acquire a new capital asset, undertake a major modification to an existing asset, or use some other method such as contracting for services [19]. More specifically, the goal of the circular is to promote efficient resource allocation through well-informed decision making by the federal government. The circular provides general guidance for conducting benefit-cost and cost-effectiveness analyses, and serves as a checklist of whether an agency has considered and properly dealt with all elements of a sound analysis.

OMB's *Capital Programming Guide* reports that credible cost and benefit analyses, such as those described in OMB Circular No. A-94, are the basis of sound management decision making, enabling agencies to determine the best investment option for meeting their goals and making them better equipped to evaluate alternatives. OMB's guide states that data are the most important piece of such analyses, including various procurement or contract data. Consequently, to do the analyses described in OMB Circular No. A-94, BOP would have to first collect and maintain comparable BOP and private facility data. BOP senior officials acknowledged that they have not done any such analyses to assess alternatives for confining inmates in low and minimum security facilities, and they were unable to explain why such analyses have not been done. Nonetheless, according to the OMB guide, selecting alternatives to meet space requirements without adequate analysis by federal agencies has resulted in higher costs than anticipated. Consequently, without such an analysis, it is difficult to know whether BOP is deciding on the most cost-effective alternative for acquiring lowand minimum security facilities to confine inmates, including whether to contract, build, or expand.

The results of any analysis conducted by BOP consistent with OMB requirements would be important because BOP officials expect inmate populations in low and minimum security facilities to rise. Inmates in low and minimum security facilities made up approximately 43 percent of BOP's total population in fiscal year 2006, and according to BOP officials, this population will continue to grow. As a result, there would be an increase of inmates requiring confinement in low and minimum security facilities. BOP also projects about a one-third increase in its long-term criminal alien population, [20] or approximately 5,700 more criminal alien inmates between fiscal years 2005 and 2008, which could further strain BOP resources as these inmates are confined primarily in low security facilities. While the private sector has additional capacity to accommodate at least some of this expected growth in inmate populations, BOP cannot determine whether private contracting is or would be the most cost- effective alternative because of the data limitations discussed above.

While there are costs associated with gathering data needed to compare costs across BOP and private facilities, without the data to conduct benefit-cost or cost-effectiveness analyses, BOP is not able to compare alternatives for confining inmates in a methodologically sound manner. Additionally, the absence of data also has potential long-term costs because BOP managers, OMB staff, and congressional decision makers do not have the information needed to weigh alternatives and make the best investment decisions. Although OMB staff told us that BOP provides several documents in accordance with the *Capital Programming Guide,* such as information about facilities in BOP's inventory and weekly reports about inmate population, OMB staff stated that it would be useful to have more and better comparison information on the cost of confining inmates in BOP and private low and minimum security facilities. They said that without such data, it is difficult to understand how BOP is making decisions on the most cost-effective way to manage and confine future inmates sentenced to low and minimum security facilities. OMB staff added that they consider contracting a viable option because it gives BOP the flexibility to immediately deal with population changes. However, according to OMB staff, they would not expect contracting to always becheaper because owning a facility may be more cost-effective in the long run. As a result, comparative analyses would be beneficial to help them better understand the long-term costs and benefits of owning versus the short-term costs and benefits of privatization.

CONCLUSIONS

Because of projections of future growth of inmate populations, BOP will need to continue to acquire additional capacity. However, deciding what to do in response to this need will be difficult because BOP does not have the data necessary to do a methodologically sound cost comparison of its various alternatives for confining inmates in low and minimum security facilities. Because contracting regulations do not require BOP to collect private facility data comparable to BOP facility data, BOP has not gathered or maintained data needed to conduct a methodologically sound cost comparison. Additionally, BOP is concerned with increased contract costs. However, BOP has not assessed the cost of collecting the data or whether the estimated costs would outweigh the benefits of having it. As a result, BOP is not in a position to meet OMB's capital planning requirements and evaluate whether contracting is more cost-effective than other alternatives, such as building new low and minimum security facilities, buying existing facilities that may be available, or expanding facilities already operated by BOP. Without such data, BOP cannot determine whether procuring prison confinement and services from private firms costs the government more or less than other confinement alternatives, as required by OMB.

RECOMMENDATION FOR EXECUTIVE ACTION

To help BOP evaluate alternatives for confining inmates in low and minimum security facilities, and recognizing that there is a cost associated with gathering and analyzing data needed to compare costs across BOP and private facilities, we recommend that the Attorney General direct the Director of BOP to develop a cost-effective way to collect comparative data on low and minimum security facilities confining inmates under BOP's custody and design and conduct methodologically sound analyses that compare the costs of confining inmates in these facilities in order to consider contracting among other alternatives for low and minimum security confinement, consistent with OMB requirements.

AGENCY COMMENTS AND OUR EVALUATION

We requested comments on a draft of this report from the Director of the Office of Management and Budget and from the Attorney General. While OMB did not provide comments, in a September 17, 2007, letter, BOP provided written comments, which are summarized below and included in their entirety in appendix II.

BOP disagreed with our recommendation and stated that it does not own or operate facilities to house solely criminal aliens. BOP also said it does not expect to receive funding to construct such low security facilities. Therefore, BOP does not believe there is value in developing data collection methods to compare costs of confining these inmates in private facilities versus other alternatives for confining inmates. BOP stated that, through open competition, it has been able to determine a fair and reasonable price for its contracts. In a related comment, BOP stated that our report does not reference that Congress has provided funds to contract out for inmate bed space but has not provided funding for new construction of low and minimum security facilities. BOP also noted that it does not currently have the capacity to confine low security criminal aliens and is dependent on private contractors to fill the gap, and, if construction funds were available for low and minimum security facilities, it would take several years before the bed space would become available. In addition, BOP noted that it is committed to contracting, in part, because OMB has directed BOP to take greater advantage of state and local governments and the private sector to meet its space requirements to confine inmates in low and minimum security facilities. With regard to the recommendation, BOP also stated that gathering data from contractors to aid in a cost comparison would have the potential to increase current contract costs at a time when BOP is facing budget constraints. Finally, BOP pointed out that an independent review conducted in 2005 which compared the operational cost of a BOP-owned, contractor-operated facility in Taft, California, with other low security BOP facilities meets the intent of our recommendation [21].

We agree that full and open competition can establish fair and reasonable costs for services provided by contractors. However, our recommendation is about selecting the most cost-effective alternative for confining inmates, not about selecting among contractors as the only alternative. We believe that developing data collection methods to determine the costs of confining inmates in low and minimum security facilities—regardless of whether those facilities are owned and operated by BOP or a contractor and regardless of whether the facility confines criminal aliens, U.S. citizens, or both—is critical to BOP's ability to evaluate the cost-effectiveness of contracting compared to other alternatives for confining inmates, such as constructing a new facility, modifying an existing facility, or acquiring military properties for prison use. OMB's *Capital Programming Guide* requires agencies to undertake the kind of comparison we are recommending in order to consider alternatives when making decisions about the acquisition of capital assets, such as prisons.

Adhering to OMB requirements better ensures that key decision makers, including OMB and Congress, have the information needed to make the most cost-effective investment decisions We recognize that BOP has not received funding to construct new low and minimum security facilities, but this does not mean that funds will not be appropriated in the future, especially if data demonstrate that this option is more cost-effective.

Without these data, BOP is not in a position to justify funding for new construction or other alternatives because BOP cannot do a methodologically sound comparison among low and minimum security facilities. With regard to BOP's comment that it currently does not have the capacity to confine criminal aliens and must rely on contracting to address capacity issues, our report noted that, according to OMB staff, contracting may be a viable option because it provides BOP the flexibility to immediately deal with population changes.

Nonetheless, OMB staff also said that they need more and better cost comparison information to help them understand the long-term costs and benefits of owning versus the short-term costs and benefits of privatization. OMB staff also stated that they would not always expect contracting to be cheaper because owning a facility may be more cost-effective over the long run, which is consistent with our past work [22].

With regard to BOP's concern that requiring comparable data from contractors could raise the cost of current contracts, our report recognized that there is a cost associated with gathering and analyzing additional data needed to compare costs across BOP and private facilities. However, BOP has not determined the cost of collecting the data or whether the estimated costs would outweigh the benefits of knowing the most cost-effective alternative for confining inmates. Without a cost- effective way to collect comparable data, BOP cannot conduct a methodologically sound cost comparison analysis that takes into account factors, such as facility characteristics and quality of service, which can differ from facility to facility. Collecting and analyzing these data would cost-effective investment decisions.

We disagree with BOP's assertion that it has met the intent of our recommendation via the 2005 study by the Center for Naval Analysis. In citing this study, BOP failed to recognize that this study does not compare the costs of various alternatives for confining inmates in low and minimum security facilities. Rather, it compares BOP-owned and -operated facilities with one BOP-owned and contractor-operated facility in Taft, California.

In addition, BOP stated it had provided detailed cost information and that it believed we would obtain comparable data from the private sector in order to conduct a methodologically sound cost comparison. As discussed throughout our report, the cost data BOP provided were not sufficient to conduct a methodologically sound cost comparison. As our report states, any comparative study of private and public prisons should not only be based on operational costs, but should also account for facility characteristics and the quality of services provided. We requested this information from the private sector.

As our report notes, private contractors do not maintain similar data, because BOP does not require them to report or collect the data it requires of its own facilities. BOP also provided technical comments, which we considered, and we have amended our report to incorporate these clarifications, where appropriate. We are sending copies of this report to the Attorney General and the Director of OMB. Copies will also be made available to others on request.

In addition, the report will be available at no charge on GAO's Web site at http://www.gao.gov. If you or your staff have any questions regarding this report, please contact me at (202) 512-6510 or larencee@gao.gov.

Contact points for our Offices of Congressional Relations and Public Affairs may be found on the last page of this report. Key contributors are listed in appendix III.

Eileen Regen Larence, Director,
Homeland Security and Justice Issues

APPENDIX I: OBJECTIVES, SCOPE, AND METHODOLOGY

Our work focused on the comparative cost of confining federal inmates in low and minimum security facilities owned by the Federal Bureau of Prisons (BOP) and privately managed facilities under contract to BOP. Specifically, our objective was to assess the feasibility of comparing the costs for confining inmates in low and minimum security facilities owned and operated by BOP with the cost to confine these inmates in private facilities and the implications this has for making decisions on low and minimum security confinement. Our work was initially designed to address Conference Report 109-272, accompanying the Science, State, Justice, Commerce, and Related Agencies Appropriations Act of 2006, [1] which directed GAO to compare the costs of confining federal inmates in low and minimum security facilities owned by BOP, privately managed facilities under contract to BOP, and local facilities or jails via intergovernmental agreements (IGA) with BOP [2]. However, during the course of our review, BOP did not renew IGAs for four facilities in Western Texas—in the cities of Big Spring and Eden, Texas, and Garza County and Reeves County, Texas—that confined 83 percent of federal inmates in IGA facilities. Although BOP has, over time, used hundreds of IGAs across the country to confine inmates on a short term basis—45 days or less—the four Texas facilities had evolved into facilities confining inmates on a long-term basis, similar to BOP-owned and -operated low and minimum security facilities. In January 2007, BOP awarded five contracts to confine inmates in facilities with approximately 10,000 beds, which are about 3,000 more beds than the capacity provided under the four IGAs [3]. According to BOP officials, BOP chose to compete the bed space associated with these agreements partly because the four Texas facilities outgrew their original purpose of confining small populations for short periods of time. BOP officials also stated that acquiring bed space via contracts rather than IGAs enhances their ability to oversee operations at the facilities. Because BOP no longer plans to use IGAs to confine inmates on a long-term basis, we shifted the focus of our review to BOP and private facilities only.

Specifically, we focused on (1) 27 BOP-owned and -operated low and minimum security facilities, and (2) 7 facilities operated by private firms under contract to BOP. Table 1 lists the 34 facilities we selected.

Table 1. List of Low and Minimum Security Facilities within our Scope

BOP low and minimum security facilities[a]	Location	Security level	Security level of adjacent facility (if
Allenwood	Pennsylvania	Low	Minimum
Ashland	Kentucky	Low	Minimum
Bastrop	Texas	Low	Minimum
Beaumont	Texas	Low	Minimum
Big Spring	Texas	Low	Minimum
Butner	North Carolina	Low	
Coleman	Florida	Low	
Elkton	Ohio	Low	Minimum
Forrest City	Arkansas	Low	Minimum
Fort Dix	New Jersey	Low	Minimum
BOP low and minimum security facilities[a]	Location	Security level	Security level of adjacent facility (if applicable)
Fort Worth	Texas	Low	
La Tuna	Texas	Low	Minimum
Lompoc	California	Low	
Loretto	Pennsylvania	Low	Minimum
Milan	Michigan	Low	
Petersburg	Virginia	Low	Minimum
Safford	Arizona	Low	
Sandstone	Minnesota	Low	
Seagoville	Texas	Low	Minimum
Texarkana	Texas	Low	Minimum

Table 1. (Continued)

BOP low and minimum security facilitiesa	Location	Security level	Security level of adjacent facility (if applicable)
Waseca	Minnesota	Low	
Yazoo City	Mississippi	Low	Minimum
Duluth	Minnesota	Minimum	
Montgomery	Alabama	Minimum	
Morgantown	West Virginia	Minimum	
Pensacola	Florida	Minimum	
Yankton	South Dakota	Minimum	
California City	California	Low	
Cibola	Arizona	Low	
Northeast Ohio	Ohio	Low	
McRae	Georgia	Low	
Moshannon Valley	Pennsylvania	Low	
Rivers	North Carolina	Low	
Taft	California	Low	Minimum

Source: BOP.

Note: The facilities included in this table confined federal inmates for fiscal years 2002 through 2006. During the early stages of our work, BOP identified the 27 BOP low and minimum security facilities listed above as those that had individual facility costs for fiscal years 2002 through 2006. However, in the later stages of our work, BOP officials clarified that 8 of the 27 facilities—Allenwood, Beaumont, Butner, Coleman, Forrest City, Lompoc, Petersburg, and Yazoo City—were part of complexes which included medium or high security facilities during some or all of this time period. Therefore, the individual costs for the low and minimum security facilities within these 8 complexes could not be isolated for fiscal years 2002 through 2006.

We did our work at BOP headquarters and the Office of Management and Budget (OMB) in Washington, D.C. We reviewed applicable laws, regulations, and studies on BOP programs, prison management, and contracting requirements [4]. We also examined available BOP and private contractor documents on the management of low and minimum security facilities. In addition, we met with BOP officials and worked with them to identify potential BOP and private facilities that could be compared considering basic criteria including inmate gender (male or female inmates, assuming that costs for programs and services might be different depending on gender) and whether cost data might be available on the individual facility level for a 5-year period covering fiscal years 2002 through 2006. In selecting low and minimum security facilities, we met with BOP officials to identify potential BOP and private facilities that could be compared over a 5-year period covering fiscal years 2002 through 2006. Our discussions with BOP officials resulted in the identification of 34 low and minimum security facilities operated by BOP and private contractors that confined federally sentenced male inmates over the 5-year period.

Several facilities were excluded from our scope because of issues with the availability of cost data for fiscal years 2002 through 2006. We excluded from our analysis those BOP low and minimum security facilities that are co-located with other facilities in a prison complex, since BOP does not isolate the costs of operating individual low and minimum security facilities located on the same campus with high and medium security facilities. Additionally, the Federal Correctional Institutions Miami, Oakdale, and Terminal Island are excluded from the list, as between November 2004 and June 2005 they were converted from medium to low security facilities so they do not have a comparable low security cost history. We did not include the competitive, private contract Reeves County Detention Center III in our study because the facility did not begin receiving federal inmates until 2007 and consequently did not have cost data associated with confining federal inmates. We also excluded the privately operated facility in Eloy, Arizona, as BOP chose to not exercise its option to continue contracting with the private operator at this facility in February 2006 and it became an Immigration and Customs Enforcement detention facility exclusively. In addition, because the private facilities do not confine female inmates or juveniles, we excluded all female and juvenile BOP facilities from our analysis, assuming that costs might be different depending on these inmate characteristics.

Once we selected facilities, we interviewed BOP procurement officials; budget officials; and officials from the Office of Research and Evaluation, Office of Policy Development and Planning, and Office of Design and Construction. We interviewed accounting, contracting, and operations officials as well as general counsel representing the seven individual prisons of the private firms. Over the course of our review, we used numerous studies as well as data from the Bureau of Justice Statistics to put together a list of variables that might affect a cost comparison analysis. Where possible, we gathered and reviewed available data on the facilities and examined whether the data would be suitable for a comparison based, in part, on key factors—such as similar facility characteristics and levels of service—needed to do a methodologically sound comparison as outlined in our 1996 report and Office of Management and Budget (OMB) Circular No. A-76: *Performance of Commercial* Activities [5]. Some studies in our 1996 report, for instance, used a variety of quality measures or outcomes such as safety, incident data, and the extent of programs available to inmates [6].

In order to determine if the selected BOP and private facilities were sufficiently similar to allow a methodologically sound comparison, we attempted to analyze facility characteristics data. In addition, we analyzed the historical costs to the government including direct (i.e., salaries, supplies, and cost of services) and indirect costs, such as support costs and operating and maintenance costs for buildings, equipment, and utilities and cost-related data between fiscal years 2002 and 2006 associated with operating low and minimum security BOP and private facilities. Additionally, we met with prison experts from Florida State University College of Criminology and Criminal Justice and from the JFA.

Institute—a nonprofit agency conducting justice and corrections research for effective policy making—to further our understanding about prisons and the complexities of comparing the costs of operating private and public prisons. We reviewed documentation on how BOP evaluates and assesses contract proposals to determine what data are used to make contracting decisions. In addition, we reviewed the Federal Acquisition Regulation to determine what requirements were applicable to BOP with respect to cost data and cost comparisons. Finally, we examined studies done to compare the cost of operating one BOP facility in Taft, California, that is owned by BOP but operated by a private contractor, as well as a study conducted by the National Academy for Public Administration on the feasibility of using low and minimum security BOP facilities to confine federal medium and high security inmates.

To assess the implications a cost comparison has for making decisions on low and minimum security facilities, we met with BOP officials and reviewed BOP population data, population projection data, and data on short-term and long-term facility planning. We also examined BOP documents within the context of OMB requirements on capital planning and space acquisition [7]. In addition, we met with OMB staff responsible for BOP budget review and preparation to discuss BOP efforts to acquire space to confine inmates in low and minimum security facilities in order to determine the information BOP provides OMB on capital investments and how this information is used to inform decisions. We also met with officials from the National Institute of Justice (NIJ) to discuss NIJ's current and past work on prison privatization and NIJ's role within the Department of Justice.

We conducted our work from May 2006 through August 2007 in accordance with generally accepted government auditing standards.

APPENDIX II:

COMMENTS FROM THE FEDERAL BUREAU OF PRISONS

U.S. Department of Justice

Federal Bureau of Prisons

Office of the Director

Washington, DC 20534

September 17, 2007

Eileen Regan Larence, Director
Homeland Security and Justice Issues
Government Accountability Office
Washington, DC 20548

Dear Ms. Larence:

The Bureau of Prisons (Bureau) appreciates the opportunity to formally respond to the Government Accountability Office's (GAO's) draft report entitled Bureau of Prisons Needs Better Data to Assess Alternatives for Acquiring Low and Minimum Security Facilities.

The purpose of the report was for the GAO to compare the costs incurred by the Bureau in operating stand-alone minimum and low security institutions to what it costs to operate private facilities or intergovernmental agreement facilities for the same type of operation. Over the course of this review, the Bureau provided GAO with considerable amounts of detailed cost comparison data for Fiscal Years 2002-2006. If the GAO staff believed that more detailed information from the private sector was needed, it was our understanding they would obtain the cost data and its basis from the private sector companies involved.

The current contracts the Bureau has in place were awarded after full and open competitions were conducted. Given the market, we believe the agency is paying a fair and reasonable cost for the services provided by the contractors.

In addition to the above general comments, we have the following specific comments:

- Page 2, paragraph 2, line 12 - Change the following wording from: "Instead, BOP awarded 5 contracts to confine..." to "Instead, the BOP conducted a full and open competition which resulted in 5 contract awards to confine inmates..."

- Page 5, paragraph 1 - The Bureau does maintain and collect sufficient data on real property owned by the Bureau. However, data is not collected on private contract facilities because the contracts are service contracts with a firm fixed rate for the care of inmates.

- Page 5, paragraph 4 - The Bureau does not collect facility data from private providers because, as stated above, the private providers have service contracts with a firm fixed rate. When private providers submit proposals, the rate includes all the costs to operate a facility. The report does not acknowledge the type of contracts involved (i.e., firm fixed price) and instead infers the Bureau does not collect this data only because it is not required.

- Page 5, paragraph 4 - The Bureau is committed to contracting out the confinement of inmates in low and minimum security facilities, as mandated by Office of Management and Budget (OMB). OMB has repeated the following direction regarding BOP "...take greater advantage of state and local and private sector bedspace to meet its space requirements..." in the FY 2006 and FY 2007 PART updates to the FY 2003 PART Improvement Plan. These updates are based on OMB's PART assessment of BOP's S&E budget. OMB has directed contracting out despite the cost evidence we have provided.

- Page 7, paragraph 1 - The Bureau's mission statement referenced should be reflected as follows:

  The BOP's mission has evolved into protecting society by controlling offenders in the controlled environments of prisons and community-based facilities that are safe, humane, cost-efficient, and appropriately secure and that provide work and other self improvement opportunities to assist offenders in becoming law-abiding citizens.

- There is no reference in the draft report indicating congressional appropriators have been committed to having the Bureau contract out (to the greatest extent possible) for bed space for minimum and low security inmates. This commitment is evidenced by the increases provided in enacted budgets for Contract Confinement, while no funding has been provided for New Prison Construction (for low and minimum security inmates) for over 14 years. Due to the continued increases in the inmate population and lack of bed space, crowding in Bureau facilities remains at high levels. The Bureau has become more and more dependent on the use of private contractors to house certain low and minimum security inmates (criminal aliens in particular).

- The Bureau does not currently have the capacity to house this particular group of inmates (low security criminal aliens) in any Bureau facility, or in the near future (2 to 5 years out). We are clearly dependent on private contractors. If funding were received to construct a low or minimum security facility, it would take at least 3 years before the bed space would become available. Meanwhile, private contractors anticipate the growing inmate populations (federal, state, local) and are continually prepared to expand their operations.

In addition to the above concerns, our response to the recommendation is as follows:

Recommendation: BOP develop a cost-effective way to collect comparative data on low and minimum security facilities confining inmates under Bureau custody and design and conduct methodologically sound analyses that compare the cost of confining inmates in these facilities in order to consider contracting among other alternatives for low and minimum security confinement, consistent with the OMB requirements.

Response: We disagree with this recommendation. The Bureau does not own or operate facilities to house solely criminal aliens and will not be receiving funding to construct such low security facilities. Accordingly, there is no value in developing data collection methods in an attempt to determine the costs of housing this particular group of inmates in a Bureau facility.

The Bureau has been able to determine what it actually costs to contract out this particular population to private contractors via open competition. In addition, we are able to determine what is fair and reasonable with regard to pricing through the use of firm fixed price contracts.

We do not see the value of requiring existing private contractors to provide specific comparable data to aid in a cost comparison. This requirement would have the potential to increase current contract costs at a time when the Bureau is facing serious budget constraints.

We believe the independent review by the Center for Naval Analysis, which compared the operational cost of the contractor-operated facility in Taft, California, with other low security BOP facilities, meets the intent of the recommendation.

3

If you have any questions regarding this response, please contact VaNessa P. Adams, Senior Deputy Assistant Director, Program Review Division, at (202) 616-2099.

Sincerely,

Harley G. Lappin
Director

cc: Richard Theis, Assistant Director
Audit Liaison Group, JMD

References

[1] IGAs are agreements between BOP and state and local governments to confine BOP inmates in state and local prison facilities.

[2] Pub. L. No. 109-108, 119 Stat. 2290 (2005).

[3] BOP awarded these five contracts on January 17, 2007.

[4] According to BOP, prison programs include services and classes that provide productive use-of-time activities and facilitate the successful reintegration of inmates into society, consistent with community expectations and standards.

[5] Because the private facilities we selected for our review do not confine female inmates or juveniles, we excluded all female and juvenile BOP facilities from our analysis

[6] GAO, *Private and Public Prisons: Studies Comparing Operational Costs and/or Quality of Service,* GAO/GGD-96-158 (Washington, D.C.: Aug. 16, 1996).

[7] Office of Management and Budget, Executive Office of the President, OMB Circular No. A-11, Part 7, *Capital Programming Guide* (2006). A benefit-cost analysis is a systematic quantitative method of weighing the costs associated with implementing or operating an alternative against any benefits expected from the alternative. A cost-effectiveness analysis is a systematic quantitative method for comparing the cost of alternatives when such alternatives achieve the same benefits. According to OMB, it is a less comprehensive technique than a benefit-cost analysis, but can be appropriate for ranking alternatives when the benefits of competing alternatives are the same. An alternative is considered cost- effective when it is determined to have the lowest cost for a given amount of benefit.

[8] Nelson, Julianne, *Competition in Corrections: Comparing Public and Private Sector Operations*, the Center for Naval Analysis Corporation (Virginia: December 2005).

[9] According to BOP, a pretrial inmate is a person who is legally detained but for whom BOP has not received notification of conviction. Thus, pretrial inmates include persons awaiting trial, being tried, or awaiting a verdict.

[10] GAO/GGD-96-158. While exploring how we would conduct a comparison for this report, we took into account factors outlined in our 1996 report on studies that compared the cost of private and public prisons to ensure that our comparison would be methodologically sound and generalizeable to federal low and minimum security facilities nationwide regardless of the operator. In addition to the factors mentioned above, our 1996 report stated that a variety

of other factors could affect a cost comparison of prison facilities such as cost-of-living and economic differences among the nation's geographic regions.

[11] Studies we reviewed identified misconduct incidences as inmate-on-inmate assaults, staffon-inmate assaults, inmate-on-staff assaults, drug and contraband violations, sexual assaults, homicides, suicides, and escapes from the facility.

[12] SENTRY is BOP's online, real-time database system, used primarily for maintaining information about federal inmates including sentencing, work assignments, admission/release status, and other special assignments for monitoring inmate status. According to contracting requirements, each private contractor is required to provide and maintain hardware and software to access SENTRY.

[13] Although we reviewed the available data maintained by BOP, for the purposes of this report, we did not assess the contractor's compliance with BOP's data entry requirements to confirm whether the private sector data were consistent with BOP's misconduct categories because BOP's monitoring and oversight of its contracts was beyond the scope of our review.

[14] Firm-fixed price contracts provide for a price that is not subject to any adjustment on the basis of the contractor's cost experience in performing the contract. This contract type places upon the contractor maximum risk and full responsibility for all costs and resulting profit or loss.

[15] Federal Acquisition Regulation, 48 C.F.R. §§ 15.305(a)(1), 15.403-1(c) (2006).

[16] GAO, *Federal Real Property: Reliance on Costly Leasing to Meet New Space Needs Is an Ongoing Problem*, GAO-06-136T (Washington, D.C.: Oct. 6, 2005), 5-8.

[17] The cost of construction was compared to the options of (1) lease-purchases in which payments are spread out over time and ownership of the asset is eventually transferred to the government, and (2) operating leases in which periodic lease payments are made over the specified length of the lease.

[18] Office of Management and Budget, Executive Office of the President, OMB Circular No. A-11, Part 7, *Capital Programming Guide* (2006).

[19] Office of Management and Budget, Executive Office of the President, OMB Circular No. A-94, *Guidelines and Discount Rates for Benefit-Cost Analysis of Federal Programs* (1992).

[20] According to BOP, long-term criminal aliens are those criminal aliens confined in low and minimum security facilities for more than 45 days.

[21] Nelson (2005).
[22] GAO-06-136T.

Appendix I

[1] Pub. L. No. 109-108, 119 Stat. 2290 (2005).
[2] IGAs are agreements between BOP and state and local governments to confine BOP inmates in state and local prison facilities.
[3] Three of the five contracts were awarded to the private firms that operated the former IGA facilities for the local governments. The fourth contract was awarded directly to the local government that owns the facility, Reeves County. BOP also awarded a fifth contract to a new contractor in Pine Prairie, Louisiana[4]According to BOP, prison programs include services and classes that provide productive use-of-time activities and facilitate the successful reintegration of inmates into society, consistent with community expectations and standards.
[4] GAO/GGD-96-158 and Office of Management and Budget, Executive Office of the President, OMB Circular No. A-76, *Performance of Commercial Activities* (2003).
[5] While we attempted to collect data to compare the level of service provided, we did not attempt to assess BOP's monitoring and oversight of its contracts as they relate to the contractor's performance and quality of service because doing so was beyond the scope of our review.
[6] Office of Management and Budget, Executive Office of the President, OMB Circular No. A-11, Part 7, *Capital Programming Guide* (2006).
[7] Office of Management and Budget, Executive Office of the President, OMB Circular No. A-11, Part 7, *Capital Programming Guide* (2006).

In: Controlling Federal Prison Costs
Editor: Gregory N. Berritas
ISBN 978-1-60692-650-5

Chapter 2

PRISON CONSTRUCTION*

ABBREVIATIONS

BOP	Bureau of Prisons
CII	Construction Industry Institute
CPC	Capacity Planning Committee
DOJ	Department of Justice
EPA	Environmental Protection Agency
FCI	Federal Correctional Institution
ICIPPI	*Inputs to Construction Industries Producer Price Index*
LRPC	Long-Range Planning Committee
OMB	Office of Management and Budget

May 29, 2008

The Honorable Barbara A. Mikulski Chairman

The Honorable Richard C. Shelby Ranking Member

Subcommittee on Commerce, Justice, Science, and Related Agencies Committee on Appropriations, United States Senate

* Excerpted from GAO Report to the Subcommittee on Commerce, Justice, Science, and Related Agencies, Committee on Appropriations, U.S. Senate, dated May 2008.

The federal Bureau of Prisons (BOP), within the Department of Justice (DOJ), is responsible for the custody and care of more than 201,000 federal offenders. To accommodate the current and future confinement needs of the U.S. federal prison population, BOP manages the construction and maintenance of its prison facilities. BOP also contracts with other facilities to house about 17 percent of the federal offenders. Cost estimates that BOP provided to Congress for BOP's three current prison construction projects that are located in Mendota, California; Berlin, New Hampshire; and McDowell, West Virginia, have increased significantly beyond the initial estimates. For the purposes of this report, we refer to these Federal Correctional Institution (FCI) construction projects as FCI Mendota, FCI Berlin, and FCI McDowell. To date, additional funding has been provided for these projects totaling almost $278 million, or 62 percent more than the projects' initial estimates.

To assist the Subcommittee in its oversight role and in making future funding decisions, you requested that we examine the circumstances surrounding the increases in the cost estimates for the three current construction projects. Accordingly, for the three prisons currently under construction, this report addresses (1) the reasons for the changes to the estimated costs to date and (2) the actions BOP has taken—or plans to take—to control future cost increases and schedule delays.

To assess the reasons for the changes to the estimated costs related to the three prisons currently under construction, we analyzed DOJ's congressional budget submissions for BOP from the first year that project funding was requested in fiscal years 2001 through 2009, and relevant appropriation laws. We also reviewed and analyzed BOP's cost estimates, project files, and capital planning guidance. We analyzed the Office of Management and Budget's (OMB) guidance on capital planning andpreparing budget submissions. In addition, to identify the rate of inflation and other price indicators that could have affected the cost estimates for the three project schedules, we analyzed the Department of Labor, Bureau of Labor Statistics, pricing indexes for 2003 through 2007, and interviewed BOP officials in Washington, D.C.

To assess the actions taken by BOP—or that BOP plans to take—to control cost increases and schedule delays on the three current construction projects, we analyzed BOP's construction guidance and BOP's project files. Furthermore, we reviewed federal government and construction industry data concerning project cost management and compared them with BOP's guidance. We also interviewed BOP headquarters officials in Washington, D.C. We discuss the scope and methodology of this report in more detail in appendix I.

We conducted this performance audit from June 2007 through May 2008, in accordance with generally accepted government auditing standards. Those standards require that we plan and perform the audit to obtain sufficient, appropriate evidence to provide a reasonable basis for our findings and conclusions based on our audit objectives. We believe that the evidence obtained provides a reasonable basis for our findings and conclusions based on our audit objectives.

RESULTS IN BRIEF

Delays in starting project construction or disruptions in available funding that interrupted construction contributed to increases in cost estimates due to inflation and unexpected increases in construction material costs. According to BOP officials, problems with selecting and approving the sites for FCI Mendota, FCI Berlin, and FCI McDowell, along with receiving funding later than assumed in the initial estimates, delayed the three prison projects. BOP officials stated that costs increased by the associated inflation that occurs over time, but BOP could not anticipate construction industry costs that increased at an accelerated rate due to other market factors. For example, steel prices rose by about 60 percent and oil prices rose by almost 170 percent from the time that BOP prepared the initial cost estimates for these projects until the projects were ready to proceed with construction. In addition, because BOP estimates its initial project costs and requests funding early in the planning process—generally, before an actual location for a prison has been selected—variance from the initial estimates would be expected to some extent, even if the projects are not delayed. BOP, like other agencies, is not required to communicate how much it expects costs might vary from its estimates in the budget documents submitted to Congress and other stakeholders. Without suchinformation, however, Congress and other stakeholders do not know the extent to which additional funding may be required to complete the project, even absent any project delays.

BOP eliminated or reduced portions of two projects to remain within the amount funded, and it plans to use its construction management policies and procedures to control further cost increases and schedule delays. When awarding the construction contract for FCI Mendota in 2007, BOP eliminated a Federal Prison Industries facility (UNICOR), which would have provided additional employment and job skills training opportunities for inmates, and the minimum-security prison camp. At FCI Berlin, BOP eliminated the UNICOR facility when it awarded the contract in 2007, but it subsequently added a smaller UNICOR facility to the project, which will be paid for by UNICOR. Although intended to reduce costs, these changes also reduced the functionality of the two prisons and deviated from what BOP planned and requested funding for. In the subsequent budget submission to Congress and other stakeholders, BOP did not clearly communicate these changes, since it does not provide such detailed project information. Now that BOP has awarded contracts to construct these three projects, BOP officials believe that their construction management policies and procedures will allow them to control cost increases and schedule delays. These policies and procedures reflect current government and industry project management practices to monitor and track projects, and to report on their status. In addition, BOP officials told us that their use of the Design-Build project delivery system will help to control cost increases during construction. Under this system, the contractor designs and builds the project and generally has the responsibility for costs associated with design errors, should they occur. Furthermore, BOP officials told us that they plan to continue to carefully consider and approve changes that would increase construction costs after construction begins. We did not evaluate the effectiveness of BOP's construction policies and procedures in controlling cost increases and schedule delays on these three projects because while design and construction contracts were awarded, little construction had been done.

To improve accountability and transparency, we are making two recommendations to the Attorney General of the United States to instruct the Director of BOP to clearly communicate the following to Congress and other stakeholders in DOJ's annual congressional budget submission, in which BOP provides its requests for funding and reports the status of construction projects: (1) the extent to which project costs might vary from initial estimates and (2) the changes that might impact the functionality of projects. BOP concurred with our recommendations.

Background

BOP's mission is to protect society by confining offenders in the controlled environments of prisons and community-based facilities that are safe, humane, cost-efficient, and appropriately secure, and that provide work and other self-improvement opportunities to assist offenders in becoming law-abiding citizens. BOP is organized into six regions of the country—Mid-Atlantic, North Central, Northeast, South Central, Southeast, and Western. BOP manages the construction of and operates institutions at five security levels—minimum, low, medium, high, or administrative security—to confine offenders in an appropriate manner. Institutions constructed for a given security level generally have the same design and features. For example, FCIs, which are medium-security institutions, generally have strengthened perimeter fencing, cell-type housing, and a wide variety of work and treatment programs. As such, FCI construction projects typically include a UNICOR facility that employs and provides job skills training to inmates [1]. UNICOR is a government corporation administered by DOJ, with the Director of the Bureau of Prisons as its Chief Executive Officer. FCI construction projects also generally include an adjacent work- and program-oriented minimum- security Federal Prison Camp, where inmates help serve the labor needs of the larger, higher-security FCI.

We have previously reported that BOP follows a centralized, long-term capacity planning process, with the aim of ensuring sufficient institutional capacity while maintaining prison populations at safe-and-secure targeted levels [2]. BOP has two planning committees that are involved in the capital decision-making process to identify new facility prison construction projects: the Capacity Planning Committee (CPC) and the Long-Range Planning Committee (LRPC) [3]. According to BOP headquarters officials, CPC proposes new projects by BOP region using the Capacity Plan, which provides projections of inmate population and rates of prison overcrowding. BOP develops initial budget estimates for the projects that CPC proposes, and LRPC ranks the proposed new prison facility construction projects and makes specific funding recommendations to the Director of BOP. The new construction projects are ranked on the basis of agency need, funding, and the speed with which the projects can be constructed.

BOP includes its proposed new construction projects in its annual Federal Prison System budget request made to DOJ. As part of the DOJ annual congressional budget submission, BOP also provides its Federal Prison System Status of Construction report (status report), which provides information on the status of construction for major projects that have received funding. The specific information provided is as follows: each project's descriptive title, with name, type, and location; the amounts funded, by fiscal year; the total project cost estimates; the funds obligated to date; the estimated year of use; and a brief status of the project. However, detailed project information is not provided in this status report. Although BOP provides information to Congress about the specific projects that it plans to support with the funds it requests, funding for BOP construction is provided as a lump sum into its "Buildings and Facilities Account," rather than by the specific project. As a result, BOP can shift funds within this account to fund cost increases on different projects.

In the last 10 years, BOP has completed 30 prison projects at a cost totaling over $3.6 billion. BOP has received about $710 million for the 3 prison projects currently under construction—FCI Mendota, FCI Berlin, and FCI McDowell. BOP has plans for 10 additional prison projects that have received about $363 million in funding to date, as listed in its fiscal year 2009 congressional budget submission [4].

Developing Initial Project Cost Estimates

To request funding for construction projects such as a prison, an agency must develop an initial project cost estimate several years before it plans to begin construction. Cost estimating requires both science and judgment. Since answers are seldom—if ever—precise, the goal is to find a reasonable "answer" [5]. Cost estimates are based on many assumptions, including the rate of inflation and when construction will begin. Generally, the more information that is known about a project and is used in the development of the estimate, the more accurate the estimate is expected to be [6]. OMB's guidance for preparing budget documents identifies many types and methods of estimating project costs. The expected accuracy of the resulting project cost estimates varies, depending on the estimating method used.

As part of the project planning and budgeting process, BOP officials develop an initial cost estimate when the need is identified for a prison in a particular region of the country. Given that its prisons for a specific security level generally have the same design features, BOP uses cost and pricing information from a previous project to create a national average cost for construction as the basis for its initial estimate of a new project. To develop an initial cost estimate, BOP adjusts its national average cost by assumptions for various factors, such as the difference in construction costs for different regions of the country, the difficulty of construction, and the expected inflation until construction is planned to begin. For example, in 1999, BOP created a national average construction cost for an FCI on the basis of the average of the 1998 bids for FCI Petersburg, Virginia, the most recently available FCI construction cost information. BOP adjusted FCI Petersburg's pricing information to take into account inflation between 1998 and 1999 and the relative construction costs in Petersburg. To establish the initial estimate for FCI Mid-Atlantic—which became FCI McDowell, located in McDowell County, West Virginia—BOP adjusted the national average to take into account the relative construction costs and difficulty of construction for the Mid-Atlantic region of the country and inflation adjustment to 2001, which is when BOP expected to begin construction. BOP used this estimate as the basis for requesting funding.

BOP's process of using cost information from an earlier project to estimate the cost of a similar proposed project is one of the types of estimates discussed in OMB's guidance. Because this type of cost estimate is based on a single overall project cost, guidance indicates that actual project costs may vary from such an estimate by as much as ± 40 percent [7]. Actual costs may vary by this percentage even if the project begins as assumed in the estimate because detailed project information, such as quantities of particular construction components, was not used in developing the estimate. A BOP official stated that he believes BOP's estimates are more accurate than ± 40 percent because it uses its own historical project information, and the similarities shared by by BOP projects.

Project Delays Contributed to Increased Cost Estimates, and the Imprecise Nature of Estimates Was Not Communicated to ongress and Other Stakeholders

Delays in starting project construction or disruptions in available funding, which interrupted construction, contributed to increases in cost estimates due to inflation and to unexpected increases in construction material costs. According to BOP officials, problems associated with selecting sites for FCI Mendota, FCI Berlin, and FCI McDowell and with receiving the funding later than planned in the initial estimates contributed to the increase in the cost estimates.

During the time that the projects were delayed, construction costs rose at a rate higher than inflation. Also, cost estimates are imprecise and should be expected to vary from initial estimates, but Congress and other stakeholders were not informed about the extent to which costs might vary from the initial estimates.

Problems with Site Selection and the Availability of Funding Contributed to Project Construction Delays

According to BOP officials, all three projects experienced delays in beginning construction because of problems associated with selecting and approving the sites for the prisons as well as with the availability of funding. FCI Mendota also experienced disruptions in available funding that led to an interruption in construction. See appendix II for project estimates, budget requests, and funding for the three projects.

FCI Mendota

In fiscal years 2001 and 2002, about $150 million was appropriated for a high-security United States Penitentiary in California as requested in the President's budget. Funding was reduced in fiscal year 2002 when BOP applied a rescission of about $5.7 million to the project. When BOP initially estimated the cost for this project, it expected the contract to be awarded in fiscal year 2001 and the construction to begin in fiscal year 2002. However, BOP did not award the contract to design and constructthe prison until fiscal year 2004. Mendota was selected as the prison site in fiscal year 2002, at which time BOP changed the project to a medium- security FCI [8]. Subsequent environment impact studies and approvals, which included review and approval by the Environmental Protection Agency (EPA), were completed in fiscal year 2004. In addition, the continued availability of funding for this project came into question in fiscal year 2004, when Congress rescinded almost $52 million of funding [9]. Furthermore, in fiscal year 2005 an amendment to the President's Budget proposed canceling $55 million from the unobligated balances in the Buildings and Facilities Account previously provided for the FCI Mendota project.

Despite this disruption in the available funding, BOP continued with the FCI Mendota project because it expected that the rescinded funds would be restored the following year. Partly as a result of the rescission, BOP officials separated the work for this project into several pieces. This decision enabled BOP to award a single contract for the project's design and construction in September 2004. The contract was structured for the contractor to begin with design and allowed BOP to decide when and what pieces of the construction would be done on the basis of the availability of funding. In December 2004, with the funding it had, BOP directed the contractor to construct the central utility plant, water tower, and general housing units. The contract required BOP to award the remaining pieces necessary to complete the facility—such as the support structures, UNICOR factory, and Federal Prison Camp—no later than 2006 or the option to do this work under the contract would expire. BOP did not exercise the contract option because it had not received additional funds. As a result, when the contractor completed its work, BOP could not house prisoners at FCI Mendota.

Figure 1 shows a comparison of the uncompleted FCI Mendota in California to the completed FCI Forest City in Arkansas.

Source: BOP.Incomplete: FCI Mendota, CA.

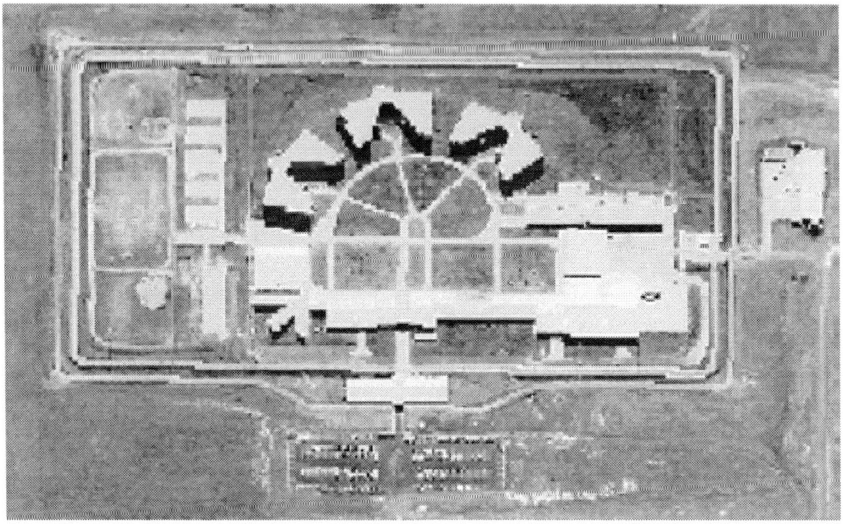

Source: United States Geological Survey.
Complete: FCI Forest City, AR

Figure 1. FCI Mendota in California and FCI Forest City in Arkansas.

Before BOP could solicit for construction bidders to complete the required work at FCI Mendota, it had to contract for additional engineering services to prepare construction documents. This was necessary to inform bidders about what work had been done and what work remained to be completed. In September 2007 after it received additional funding, BOP awarded the contract to complete FCI Mendota.

We have previously raised concerns about this type of construction management. For example, we have reported that nonconcurrent construction—that is where different phases of a project are constructed at different times—increases the overall cost to the government because it requires additional and expensive mobilization of contractor staff and equipment, security, work to procure building materials, and construction management oversight [10]. We also have raised concerns in prior work about starting capital projects without all of the funding necessary to complete the project or, if the project is divisible into stages, to complete a standalone stage that would result in a useable asset [11]. While BOP had funding for the pieces for which it awarded a contract, the pieces did not result in a usable asset because it did not have enough of the pieces of the project completed to house prisoners safely and securely. Although BOP shifted some funds to help pay for the Mendota project, according to BOP officials, sufficient funds were not available to fully fund the Mendota project without delaying or canceling other projects that BOP had told Congress it planned to begin.

To date, the total funding for FCI Mendota has exceeded the initial fiscal year 2001 estimate by about $72 million, or almost 45 percent. However, the latest project estimate is over $6 million, or 2.8 percent, more than the current funding. BOP officials have told us that they do not plan to request any more funding for this project, and that BOP will shift funds within its Buildings and Facilities Account as necessary to complete FCI Mendota.

FCI Berlin and FCI McDowell

In fiscal year 2004, about $154 million was appropriated for FCI Berlin, and about $40 million was appropriated for an FCI in the Mid-Atlantic region [12]. When BOP initially estimated the costs for these projects, it expected to receive funding for design and construction of these facilities in fiscal years 2004 and 2002, respectively. BOP did not award contracts for the design and construction of these projects until fiscal years 2007 and 2006, respectively. According to BOP, both projects experienced delays in selecting the locations for the prisons and the environment impact studies. For FCI Berlin, the property was acquired and EPA completed its approval process in fiscal year 2007.

For FCI McDowell, these events occurred in fiscal years 2006 and 2005. In addition, BOP officials stated that they were reluctant to proceed with construction because of OMB's moratorium on new construction for fiscal years 2005 through 2007. Also, the President's Budget included proposed cancellations of unobligated funds from BOP's Buildings and Facilities Account for fiscal years 2004, 2006, and 2007 [13].

To date, the total funding for FCI Berlin and FCI McDowell has exceeded the initial estimates by about $93.5 million and $112.3 million, or 56 percent and 89 percent, respectively. However, the latest project estimates are more than $11 million and $9 million, or 4.2 percent and 3.7 percent, more than the current funding for FCI Berlin and FCI McDowell, respectively. BOP officials told us that they do not plan to request any more funding for these projects, and that BOP will shift funds within its Buildings and Facilities Account as necessary to complete them.

Construction Costs Increased at a Rate Higher Than the Rate of Inflation

BOP factors into its estimates the project's expected start date and duration, on the basis of when BOP expects to receive funding. Generally, if a project does not start as assumed in the cost estimate, the estimated cost of the project should be expected to change at least by the rate of inflation that occurs during the time that elapses between the expected start date and the actual start date. BOP officials stated that during the time that these projects were delayed, construction industry costs increased at a rate greater than inflation.

Costs for materials used in construction, such as concrete, steel, copper, and oil, rose substantially. For example, steel prices rose by about 60 percent and oil prices rose by almost 150 percent between 2003 and 2007—a time between when the initial cost estimates were prepared and when the projects were ready to proceed with construction [14].

We analyzed national data on construction material costs from 2003 through 2007 to provide some context on increases to construction prices. Specifically, to identify nationwide trends in the costs of many of the materials used in construction—from concrete to electrical equipment— we analyzed the Department of Labor, Bureau of Labor Statistics' *Inputs to Construction Industries Producer Price Index* (ICIPPI) [15].

As shown in table 1, from 2003 through 2007, the ICIPPI increased more than the consumer price index, indicating that construction costs increased at a higher rate than other costs [16].

Table 1. Bureau of Labor Statistics' Indexes

	Consumer Price Index-All Urban Consumers		Producer Price Index-Inputs to Construction Industries	
Fiscal year	CPI	Percentage increase	ICIPPI	Percentage increase
2003	185.0	2.0%	142.4	3.2%
2004	190.9	3.2	156.6	10.0
2005	199.2	4.3	170.1	8.6
2006	201.8	1.3	175.6	3.2
2007	208.9	3.5	182.4	3.9
Total[a]		12.9%		28.1%

Source: GAO analysis of Department of Labor, Bureau of Labor Statistics, data.
[a]To align with the federal government fiscal year, we compared October data.

Cost Estimates Are Imprecise, and Congress and Other Stakeholders Were Not Informed of the Extent to Which They Might Vary

Because BOP estimates its initial project costs and requests funding early in the planning process, generally before the specific location for the prison has been selected, actual project costs can be expected to vary from the initial estimates to some extent.

This variance would be in addition to any cost implications of a change in the project, such as a delay in beginning construction. As we have previously noted in this report, the extent to which one might expect actual costs to vary from estimates typically depends on the type of estimating process used.

In developing its initial estimate prior to the selection of a site for the prison, BOP relies on the cost of a previous prison as the foundation of its estimate. However, BOP has more detailed information available than just the cost of a previous prison, which, if used, would likely result in a more accurate estimate. For example, BOP could analyze the design documents or itemized costs that contractors on previous projects included in their bills. In addition, when the project sites have been selected, actual local market pricing for labor and material costs could be used [17]. More BOP resources would be needed to develop such an analysis.

According to government guidance, BOP's method of using total cost information from a prior project as the basis for its estimate may result in actual project costs varying from the estimate by as much as ± 40 percent. A BOP official stated that BOP's estimating method results in more precise estimates than ± 40 percent, but an analysis of the accuracy of BOP's estimating method has not been done.

Regardless of the estimating method used, Congress relies on information provided by agencies when making funding decisions. Although BOP, like other agencies, is not required to communicate the extent to which actual costs may be expected to vary from its estimates in budget documents or reports on project status, we have recently identified providing such information as a best practice [18]. BOP has not provided this information to Congress and other stakeholders. Thus, BOP has not alerted them of the risks that BOP might require additional funding to complete the projects as originally planned.

OMB guidance points out that estimating inaccuracy—both overestimating and underestimating—can adversely affect other projects. With overestimating, an agency may request and be provided with more resources than it will actually need for the project, thereby resulting in less resources being available for other projects or programs. Underestimating projects can lead an agency to request less resources than it will actually need to complete the project, potentially leading to a significant reduction in the project scope, termination of the project, or the shifting of funds from other projects.

Inaccurate estimates also reduce confidence in the accuracy of future estimates provided by an agency. Consequently, BOP's ability to inform Congress and other stakeholders about the extent to which costs may vary from its initial project cost is important as it plans additional prison projects and submits subsequent funding requests.

BOP Has Eliminated or Reduced Portions of Two Projects, and Plans to Use Its Construction Management Policies Procedures to Control Cost and Schedule Changes

BOP eliminated or reduced portions of two projects, but did not clearly communicate these changes to Congress and other stakeholders. BOP also plans to use its construction management policies and procedures to control cost increases and schedule delays during construction.

BOP Has Eliminated or Reduced Facilities at FCI Berlin and FCI Mendota, but Did Not Clearly Communicate These Changes to Congress and Other Stakeholders

Congress appropriated funds for fiscal year 2007 that BOP indicated in its status report were required to complete the three prison projects. However, BOP eliminated portions of the FCI Berlin and FCI Mendota projects when it awarded contracts in May and September 2007, respectively, to keep the projects within the estimated costs provided to Congress. According to BOP officials, the contractors' bids for FCI Berlin and FCI Mendota were higher than expected. In response, at FCI Berlin, BOP chose to eliminate the UNICOR facility where inmates were to be employed and provided with job skills training. Subsequently, UNICOR has agreed to pay for the cost of constructing a smaller than originally planned facility, which has now been added back to the project. At FCI Mendota, BOP eliminated both the UNICOR facility and the minimum security Federal Prison Camp. Eliminating or reducing the UNICOR facilities affects BOP's mission to provide work and other self-improvement opportunities for inmates. As a result, these two projects are no longer the same as those for which BOP initially sought and received appropriated funds.

While eliminating or reducing portions of two projects enabled BOP to award contracts, the resulting facilities will not provide the same range of services as originally planned. As part of its annual congressional budget submission, BOP reports on the status of projects that have received funding in the past. This status report includes the following information: each project's descriptive title, with name, type, and location; the amounts funded, by fiscal year; the total project cost estimates; the funds obligated to date; the estimated year of use; and a brief status of the project. However, detailed project information is not provided in this status report. In reviewing the BOP Status of Construction report in DOJ fiscal year 2009 budget documents, we found that the report does not discuss theelimination of the UNICOR facility at FCI Mendota [19]. Furthermore, BOP did not mention that the Federal Prison Camp had been eliminated from FCI Mendota. The only indication of this change is that the project title no longer includes the words "with camp." While BOP receives a lump-sum appropriation for prison construction, Congress makes its appropriation on the basis of, among other things, the project information provided by BOP in its annual congressional budget submission. For FCI Berlin and FCI Mendota, BOP did not clearly communicate to Congress or other stakeholders that the facilities being constructed differed from those for which funds were requested and appropriated [20]. In addition, if BOP should decide to construct these omitted facilities in the future and fulfill these projects' initial designs, it would likely cost more than if the facilities had been constructed as one project. We have previously reported that nonconcurrent construction of a project increases the overall cost to the government because such construction requires additional and the contract to evaluate the extent to which BOP can hold the contractor reasonably liable and, therefore, responsible for the resulting costs [21]. To accomplish these tasks, BOP's *Construction Management Guidelines* provides additional guidance, which identifies the processes that BOP staff must follow to monitor the requirements and implementation of BOP construction projects. For example, this guidance requires BOP officials and the contractor to hold numerous design and construction meetings throughout the duration of the project's schedule to ensure good communication and effective management of the project.

In addition, the *Construction Management Guidelines* requires specific reports—including weekly status reports, monthly project progress reports, performance evaluations of the contractor's team members, and other reports—to facilitate oversight and monitoring of the projects within BOP. For example, this guidance requires the use of critical path method scheduling that breaks a project down into a sequence of necessary activities, which are placed into a project schedule that the project manager can closely monitor. With this management tool, BOP has the ability to monitor and track a project's current progression of work in relation to its initial schedule. This tool also gives the project manager the ability to evaluate proposed construction changes or modifications to the project and to understand their resulting impacts on the project's schedule. This evaluation step remains crucial because once BOP awards the contract, any construction changes that impact the project schedule may also lead to cost changes.

BOP's guidance establishes clear lines of responsibility and documentation requirements. The bureau's *Construction Management Guidelines* also outlines a detailed process that BOP must follow to manage and approve any changes or contract modifications to the project. For example, this guidance states that BOP's project manager should review any proposed changes or modifications to the project and determine if the changes or modifications need further review by BOP's Design and Construction Branch chief. If further review is warranted, sufficient background information supporting the changes or modifications should be provided to the branch chief, along with the proposal. In addition, this guidance states that all change or modification proposals should be discussed at regularly scheduled—or specially expensive (1) mobilization of contractor staff and equipment, (2) security, (3) work to procure building materials, and (4) construction management oversight.

BOP Plans to Use Its Policies and Procedures to Control Cost Increases and Schedule Delays during Construction

BOP officials told us that they will have more ability to control project costs because they have awarded design and construction contracts for the three projects. These officials believe that using their construction management policies and procedures will allow them to control cost increases and schedule delays. Controlling schedule delays is critical because such delays can lead to cost increases. BOP officials said they will use their *Design and Construction Procedures* and *Construction Management Guidelines* to manage the construction of prison projects. Within BOP, the Design and Construction Branch is responsible for the oversight and management of prison construction, and each project has a BOP project manager.

BOP's *Design and Construction Procedures* outlines the specific tasks that the Design and Construction Branch must complete to manage the coordination, execution, oversight, and monitoring of the activities required to construct the projects. For example, this guidance states that the project manager must monitor and report on the contractor's performance during construction and review changes or a modification to the contract to evaluate the extent to which BOP can hold the contractor reasonably liable and, therefore, responsible for the resulting costs.[21] To accomplish these tasks, BOP's *Construction Management Guidelines* provides additional guidance, which identifies the processes that BOP staff must follow to monitor the requirements and implementation of BOP construction projects. For example, this guidance requires BOP officials and the contractor to hold numerous design and construction meetings throughout the duration of the project's schedule to ensure good communication and effective management of the project.

In addition, the *Construction Management Guidelines* requires specific reports—including weekly status reports, monthly project progress reports, performance evaluations of the contractor's team members, and other reports—to facilitate oversight and monitoring of the projects within BOP. For example, this guidance requires the use of critical path method scheduling that breaks a project down into a sequence of necessary activities, which are placed into a project schedule that the project manager can closely monitor. With this management tool, BOP has the ability to monitor and track a project's current progression of work in relation to its initial schedule. This tool also gives the project manager the ability to evaluate proposed construction changes or modifications to the project and to understand their resulting impacts on the project's schedule. This evaluation step remains crucial because once BOP awards the contract, any construction changes that impact the project schedule may also lead to cost changes.

BOP's guidance establishes clear lines of responsibility and documentation requirements. The bureau's *Construction Management Guidelines* also outlines a detailed process that BOP must follow to manage and approve any changes or contract modifications to the project. For example, this guidance states that BOP's project manager should review any proposed changes or modifications to the project and determine if the changes or modifications need further review by BOP's Design and Construction Branch chief. If further review is warranted, sufficient background information supporting the changes or modifications should be provided to the branch chief, along with the proposal. In addition, this guidance states that all change or modification proposals should be discussed at regularly scheduled—or specially scheduled—progress meetings with the contractor. If the changes or modifications will affect the work, more detailed information should be provided to justify them, and the project management team must also evaluate them to ensure they are in compliance with BOP's contract requirements. Furthermore, to document the process, the guidance requires that detailed files be created and maintained for all changes or modifications.

We found that BOP's construction guidance—specifically, its *Design and Construction Procedures* and *Construction Management Guidelines*—generally conform to government and industry management practices. We compared BOP's existing construction management policies and procedures with existing guidance from OMB, [22] the General Services Administration's *Construction Excellence Features*, the Department of Energy's *Project Management for the Acquisition of Capital Assets*, and the Construction Industry Institute's (CII) *Guidelines for Implementation of CII Concepts: Best Practices for the Construction Industry* [23]. Our review showed that BOP's construction management policies and procedures required systems for monitoring, tracking, analyzing, forecasting, and reporting the status of a project. For example, we found that BOP has procedures for reporting important project information—such as cost and schedule, and their deviations from trends—to the appropriate personnel, including management. Furthermore, BOP has procedures for corrective actions when deviations in cost and schedule occur as well as procedures for controlling project changes or modifications.

In addition to the guidance, BOP officials said that the use of the Design-Build delivery system for two of these projects will help to reduce the risk of additional costs being incurred during construction [24]. This type of project delivery system places the project design and construction under one contract. This can reduce the risk of design errors being identified during construction and leading to project delays or cost increases. To provide some context to the extent that Design-Build contracting is effective in managing construction, we reviewed the National Institute of Standards and Technology and the CII study of the performance of the Design-Build delivery method versus the traditional Design-Bid-Build delivery system [25]. The study found that for maintaining the project's schedule, as well as for managing any changes or rework needed during the project's construction, when the project was managed by its owner the Design-Build system performed better than the Design-Bid-Build system.

BOP officials stated that they have more ability to control costs while the project is under construction, and that for the FCI Mendota, FCI Berlin, and FCI McDowell prison projects, they plan to continue to carefully consider and approve changes after construction has begun to stay within its budget. Since construction of the projects has just begun, it is too early to evaluate the effectiveness of BOP's construction policies and procedures in controlling cost increases and schedule delays.

CONCLUSIONS

When BOP asks Congress or other stakeholders to fund or support projects, it is important for them to be aware of the extent to which actual project costs may vary from the initial estimate. Given the continual competition for limited funds, understanding that a proposed project may need an additional 30 percent in funding as opposed to an additional 10 percent may influence their approval and funding decisions. In addition, BOP is developing its estimates and requests funding on the basis of the various facilities it intends to include in each project. If elements of a proposed and funded project that can affect its functionality are eliminated, the project may not fulfill decision makers' expectations. In addition, later construction of the omitted facilities would likely cost more than if they had been constructed as one project.

As the need for prison space continues to grow, BOP's ability to complete projects within budget and with the elements initially anticipated will be important to demonstrating BOP's ability to manage its construction program. By providing information on the accuracy of its cost estimates and clearly communicating changes that could impact the projects functionality, BOP would establish more accountability and transparency to its stakeholders.

RECOMMENDATIONS FOR EXECUTIVE ACTION

To improve accountability and transparency, we are making two recommendations to the Attorney General of the United States to instruct the Director of BOP to clearly communicate to Congress and other stakeholders in DOJ's annual congressional budget submission, in which BOP provides its requests for funding and reports on the status of construction projects:

- the extent to which project costs may vary from initial estimates and
- changes that may impact the functionality of projects.

AGENCY COMMENTS

We provided a draft of this report to the Department of Justice for its review and comment. The Director of the Federal Bureau of Prisons provided written comments on this draft. BOP concurred with our recommendations and stated it would incorporate information on the extent to which project costs may vary from initial estimates and changes that may impact the functionality of projects in DOJ's annual congressional budget submission. BOP also provided technical corrections, which we incorporated in this report where appropriate. BOP's comments are reproduced in appendix III.

We will send copies of this report to the appropriate congressional committees and the Attorney General of the United States. Additional copies will be sent to interested congressional committees and the Director of the Office of Management and Budget. We will also make copies available to others upon request. The report will be available at no charge on the GAO Web site at http://www.gao.gov.

If you have any questions about this report, please contact me at (202) 512-6923 or at dornt@gao.gov. Contact points for our Offices of Congressional Relations and Public Affairs may be found on the last page of this report. GAO staff who made key contributions to this report are listed in appendix IY.

Terrell Dorn
Director, Physical Infrastructure Issues

APPENDIX I: OBJECTIVES, SCOPE, AND METHODOLOGY

To assess the extent to which costs changed for the three prisons currently under construction and the reasons for those changes, we obtained and analyzed the President's budgets, the Department of Justice's budget justifications for the federal Bureau of Prisons (BOP) for fiscal years 2001 through 2009, and appropriation laws for fiscal years 2001 through 2008. We obtained and analyzed BOP's project files for three Federal Correctional Institution (FCI) construction projects in Mendota, California; Berlin, New Hampshire; and McDowell, West Virginia. To determine the rate of inflation and other price indicators for the duration of the three projects' schedules, we obtained and analyzed the following Department of Labor, Bureau of Labor Statistics' data: (1) *Producer Price Index-Commodities, Metals and metal products, Steel mill products*; (2) P*roducer Price Index-Commodities, Fuels and related products and power, Crude petroleum (domestic production)*; (3) *Producer Price Index Industry Data, Inputs to construction industries*; and (4) *Consumer Price Index-All Urban Consumers*. We obtained and analyzed (1) BOP's initial cost estimates for FCI Mendota, FCI Berlin, and FCI McDowell and (2) information on prison projects completed from 1998 to 2007—10 years prior to our review—to learn about BOP historical costs. We reviewed BOP's capital planning guidance. We obtained and analyzed the Office of Management and Budget's (OMB) guidance for Capital Planning and Budget Submission. We interviewed BOP construction, budget, and financial officials in Washington, D.C.

To assess the actions BOP has taken—or plans to take—to control cost increases and schedule delays on the three current construction projects, we obtained and analyzed BOP's construction guidance and BOP's project files for FCI Mendota, FCI Berlin, and FCI McDowell. We obtained and analyzed government and construction industry data concerning project cost management and guidance from OMB's Circular A-11, the General Services Administration's *Construction Excellence Features*, the Department of Energy's *Project Management for the Acquisition of Capital Assets*, and the Construction Industry Institute's (CII) *Best Practices for the Construction Industry.* We obtained and analyzed government and construction industry data concerning the performance of the Design-Build delivery method versus the traditional Design-Bid-Build delivery system from the National Institute of Standards and Technology and the CII study. We interviewed BOP construction, budget, and financial officials in Washington, D.C. We did not evaluate the effectiveness of BOP's construction policies and procedures in controlling cost increases and schedule delays on these projects because although design and construction contracts were awarded, little construction had been doneWe conducted this performance audit from June 2007 through May 2008, in accordance with generally accepted government auditing standards. Those standards require that we plan and perform the audit to obtain sufficient, appropriate evidence to provide a reasonable basis for our findings and conclusions based on our audit objectives. We believe that the evidence obtained provides a reasonable basis for our findings and conclusions based on our audit objectives.

APPENDIX II: FCI MENDOTA, FCI BERLIN, AND FCI MCDOWELL: PROJECT ESTIMATES, BUDGET REQUESTS, AND FUNDING FOR FISCAL YEARS 2001–2009

Dollars in thousands	**Prison construction project**		
Fiscal year/Project information category	**FCI Mendota**	**FCI Berlin**	**FCI McDowell**
2001			
Estimate	$1 58,930[a]	N/A	$1 26,430[a]
Request	11,930	N/A	5,430
Funded	8,930	N/A	2,430
2002			
Estimate	158,930	$1 66,000[a]	126,430
Request	147,000	9,963	91,047
Funded	141 ,256[b]	5,000	94,047
2003			
Estimate	158,930	173,039	131,314
Request	0[c]	0[c]	0[c]
Funded	0[c]	20,000	0c
2004			
Estimate	150,186	179,500	136,777
Request	0[c]	Cancellation[d]	Cancellation[d]
Funded	(48,895)[e]	154,500	40,300
2005			
Estimate	150,186	179,500	136,777

Table (Continued)

Fiscal year/Project information category	Prison construction project		
	FCI Mendota	**FCI Berlin**	**FCI McDowell**
Request	(55,000)	0[c]	0[c]
Funded	1,900	0[c]	0[c]
2006			
Estimate	165,291	179,500	136,777
Request	0[c]	Cancellation[d]	Cancellation[d]
Funded	4,000	0[c]	0[c]
2007			
Estimate	196,291	179,500	136,777
Request	0[c]	Cancellation[d]	Cancellation[d]
Funded	122,050	80,000	102,000
2008			
Estimate	225,000 to 235,000	250,000 to275,000	225,000 to 235,000
Request	115,000	0[c]	0[c]
Funded	2,000	0 c	0c
2009			
Estimate	238,000	271,000	248,000
Request	0c	0c	0c
Funded	f	f	f
Total funding	$231,241	$259,500	$238,777
Minus initial estimate	158,903	166,000	126,430
Dollar increase	$72,311	$93,500	$112,347
Percentage increase	45%	56%	89%

Source: GAO analysis of Department of Justice, Bureau of Prisons, data.

Note: In the President's fiscal year 2005 budget, a moratorium on new prison construction was announced. This moratorium was in place for fiscal years 2005, 2006, and 2007.

[a]initial estimate of project costs.

[b]Includes a rescission to the Buildings and Facilities Account of $5.744 million, which was applied by BOP.

[c]The use of "zeros" indicates either no budget requests or no project funding.

[d]The term "cancellation" refers to a proposal by the President to reduce budget resources.

[e]The Appropriation Conference Report named the project, which became FCI Mendota, to apply the rescission to the Buildings and Facilities Account. In fiscal year 2004, BOP shifted $3 million to this project.

[f]Fiscal year 2009 funds have not been determined.

Appendix III: Comments from the Department of Justice, Federal Bureau of Prisons

U.S. Department of Justice

Federal Bureau of Prisons

Office of the Director

Washington, DC 20534

May 16, 2008

Terrell Dorn, Director
Physical Infrastructure Issues
Government Accountability Office
Washington, DC 20548

Dear Mr. Dorn:

The Bureau of Prisons (Bureau) appreciates the opportunity to formally respond to the Government Accountability Office's (GAO's) draft report entitled Prison Construction: Clear Communication on the Accuracy of Cost Estimates and Project Changes Needed.

The purpose of this report is to explain (1) the reasons for the changes to the estimated costs for federal correctional institution construction projects located in Mendota, California; Berlin, New Hampshire; and McDowell, West Virginia; and (2) the actions the Bureau has taken - or plans to take - to control future costs and schedule changes.

The Bureau has the following specific comments:

- Summary Page - The GAO Report should note the Status of Construction Exhibit (in the Bureau's budget) does not normally discuss specific details regarding various program areas of each prison project - such as UNICOR work areas.
- Page 3, 2nd paragraph and thereafter - We suggest the following wording change be included: "Inmates are employed in many areas of BOP institutions (food service, commissary, facility maintenance, landscaping/grounds work, barber shop, cleaning, etc.) not just UNICOR." The GAO's current statement might lead the reader to believe there will be no work opportunities for inmates at these locations without a UNICOR operation. In fact, all sentenced general population BOP inmates at all locations are required to work and are given a job if they are medically able.

- Page 4, 9th line beginning with, "Furthermore,..." - We suggest the sentence should read, "Furthermore, BOP officials told us they will continue to carefully consider and analyze before approving changes that would increase construction costs after construction begins."

- Page 5, 6th line from the top beginning with, "UNICOR is a..." - We suggest the sentence read, "The Director of the Federal Prison System, Chief Executive Officer, and a board of six Directors, appointed by the President, reviews and approves the policy of the Corporation."

- Page 6, footnote #3: Add the underlined words to the footnote "One of the ten, a <u>secure female</u> FCI to be built in Aliceville, AL,..."

- Page 8, Title - <u>Project Delays Contributed to Increased Cost Estimates and Imprecise Nature of Estimates Not Communicated to Stakeholders</u>, we suggest replacing "Project Delays" with "Delays Related to Funding".

- Middle of Page 8, Title - <u>Problems with site selection and receiving funding later then planned contributed to project construction delays</u> we suggest replacing then with than.

- Page 8, 2nd paragraph beginning with, "FCI Mendota also experienced..." Change to make more accurate/precise, "FCI Mendota also experienced a number of disruptions in available funding including proposals for and actual rescissions of funds that led to delays and an interruption in construction."

- Page 8, end of 2nd paragraph, please add, "For example, the Administration offered a FY 2005 Budget Amendment to rescind $55 million from the Mendota project, which was eventually denied in Congressional action (Attachment 4).

- Page 9, top of page where the 2004 rescission is referenced, please include the FY 2002 rescission amount of $5.744 million which was applied to the Mendota project.

- Page 11, 1st paragraph, 8th line, containing "...EPA completed its approval process ..." Instead of EPA, we suggest... "the environmental review and approval process was completed..."

- Page 11 and Appendix II beginning with, "Also, the President's Budget..." The OMB did call these rescissions in the budget documents and only clarified, after submission of the FY 2007 President's Budget, that they were proposed cancellations (Attachment 1).
- Page 16, Line 8, "For FCIs Berlin and Mendota, BOP did not clearly communicate..." Changes are included in the Status of Construction Report which shows any planned satellite camp right after the name of the project. The Bureau did clearly change this on the Status report (Attachment 3) that went to all shareholders after award of the construction contract that did not include the camp.
- Page 23, table should be updated to reflect FY 2002 rescission of $5.744 million applied to the Mendota project. Further, budget documents (Attachment 2) clearly state "rescinds" not "cancel" for projects prior to FY 2007. The table should be updated to reflect this issue. In addition, as agreed upon in George Depaoli's May 6, 2008, e-mail, please correct the FY 2005 Request Line entry and identify the $55 million Mendota rescission proposal in the Administration's budget amendment (Attachment 4).

In addition to the above concerns, our response to the Recommendations for Executive Action is as follows:

Recommendations: To improve accountability and transparency, we are making two recommendations to the Attorney General to instruct the Director of the BOP to clearly communicate to Congress and other stakeholders in DOJ's annual congressional budget submission, in which BOP provides its requests for funding and reports on the status of construction projects:

- the extent to which project costs may vary from initial estimates; and
- changes that may impact the functionality of projects.

Response: The Bureau concurs with these recommendations and will incorporate these elements into the next required DOJ annual congressional budget submission.

3

If you have any questions regarding this response, please contact VaNessa P. Adams, Senior Deputy Assistant Director, Program Review Division, at (202) 616-2099.

Sincerely,

Thomas R. Kane

for Harley G. Lappin
Director

Attachments

cc: Richard Theis, Assistant Director
Audit Liaison Group, JMD

REFERENCES

[1] BOP provides job opportunities for inmates in many areas of the institutions, including food service, commissary, facility maintenance, landscaping/grounds work, barber shop, and cleaning. The general population BOP inmates are required to work and are given a job, if they are medically able.

[2] GAO, *Budget Issues: Agency Implementation of Capital Planning Principles Is Mixed*, GAO-04-138 (Washington, D.C.: Jan. 16, 2004).

[3] CPC consists of senior-executive-level staff of several BOP divisions and subject matter experts from the Administration Division. LRPC consists of members of the Administration Division who are senior-executive-level staff, senior managers, and branch chiefs.

[4] One of these 10 planned prison projects, a secure female FCI to be built in Aliceville, Alabama, received funding for construction in fiscal year 2008. We did not include this FCI in our review because it had not received construction funding at the time that we started our work in June 2007.

[5] GAO, *Cost Assessment Guide: Best Practices for Estimating and Managing Program Costs, Exposure Draft,* GAO-07-1134SP (Washington, D.C.: July 2007).

[6] Office of Management and Budget, *Planning, Budgeting, Acquisition, and Management of Capital Assets*, OMB Circular A-11, Part 7, Section 300, "Planning, Budgeting, Acquisition, and Management of Capital Assets," Supplement to Part 7, "Capital Programming Guide" (Washington, D.C.: June 2006); and GAO-07-1134SP.

[7] OMB Circular A-11, Part 7, refers to the Department of Energy's "Cost Estimating Guide," DOE G 4301.1-1 (Washington, D.C.: Mar. 28, 1997).

[8] BOP identified Mendota, California, as the site for this prison in its budget documents in fiscal year 2006.

[9] In fiscal year 2004, Congress rescinded $51,895,000 of the unobligated balances available for Federal Prison System, Buildings and Facilities. The conference report indicated that the rescission was to apply from prior year unobligated balances originally made available for the FCI California prison construction project. H.R. Conf. Rep. No. 108-401, at 646 (2003) accompanying Pub. L. No. 108-199, 118 STAT. 3, 106 (2004).

[10] GAO, *Embassy Construction: Achieving Concurrent Construction Would Help Reduce Costs and Meet Security Goals*, GAO-04-952 (Washington, D.C.: Sept. 24, 2004).

[11] GAO, *Budget Issues: Alternative Approaches to Finance Federal Capital,* GAO-03-1011 (Washington, D.C.: Aug. 21, 2003).

[12] McDowell, West Virginia, was selected by BOP in fiscal year 2005 and was identified in BOP's budget documents as FCI McDowell beginning in fiscal year 2007.

[13] GAO, *Status of Funds Proposed for Cancellation in the President's Fiscal Year 2007 Budget*, GAO-B-308011 (Washington, D.C.: Aug. 4, 2006).

[14] Department of Labor, Bureau of Labor Statistics, *Producer Price Index-Commodities, Metals and metal products, Steel mill products*, Series ID WPU1017 (Washington, D.C.: Nov. 15, 2007); and *Producer Price Index-Commodities, Fuels and related products and power, Crude petroleum (domestic production)*, Series ID WPU056 (Washington, D.C.: Nov. 15, 2007).

[15] Department of Labor, Bureau of Labor Statistics, *Producer Price Index Industry Data, Inputs to construction industries,* Series ID PCUBCON—BCON (Washington, D.C.: Nov. 15, 2007).

[16] Department of Labor, Bureau of Labor Statistics, *Consumer Price Index-All Urban Consumers,* Series ID CUUR0000SA0 (Washington, D.C.: Nov. 15, 2007).

[17] Office of Management and Budget, *Planning, Budgeting, Acquisition, and Management of Capital Assets*, OMB Circular A-11, Part 7, Section 300, "Planning, Budgeting, Acquisition, and Management of Capital Assets," Supplement to Part 7, "Capital Programming Guide" (Washington, D.C.: June 2006); and GAO-07-1134SP.

[18] GAO-07-1134SP.

[19] This is the first report submitted after the construction contracts were awarded in 2007 for FCI Berlin and FCI Mendota, and after the decision to eliminate portions of the projects was made.

[20] According to a BOP official, stakeholders within BOP, DOJ, and OMB are advised by BOP staff of significant changes and receive a monthly updated copy of the status report.

[21] For the technical discussion of change orders and modifications, see the Federal Acquisition Regulation, Part 43, Contract Modifications.

[22] For the technical discussion of change orders and modifications, see the Federal Acquisition Regulation, Part 43, Contract Modifications.

[23] Office of Management and Budget, *Planning, Budgeting, Acquisition, and Management of Capital Assets*, OMB Circular A-11, Part 7, Section 300, "Planning, Budgeting, Acquisition, and Management of Capital Assets,"

Supplement to Part 7, "Capital Programming Guide" (Washington, D.C.: June 2006).

[24] Construction Industry Institute, *Guidelines for Implementation of CII Concepts: Best Practices for the Construction Industry,* Special Publication 42-2 (Austin, TX: September 1995).

[25] The Design-Build delivery system was not used for the current FCI Mendota construction phase.

[26] United States Department of Commerce, Technology Administration, National Institute of Standards and Technology, Office of Applied Economics, Building and Fire Research Laboratory, *Measuring the Impacts of the Delivery System on Project Performance— Design-Build and Design-Bid-Build* (Gaithersburg, MD: November 2002).

INDEX

A

B

C

D

E

F

M

N

O

P

Q

R

S

T

U

V

W